Canoe Racing

The Competitor's Guide To Marathon and Downriver Canoe Racing

Peter Heed
&
Dick Mansfield

Acorn Publishing
Box 7067
Syracuse, New York 13261

Cover photograph was taken at the start of the C-2 Men's Master Cruiser race at the 1991 U.S.C.A. National Marathon Canoe Championships — Marinette, Wisconsin. In the foreground is the team of bow paddler Cap Allen and stern paddler John Edwards (not shown). Photograph by Carl Caylor.

Library of Congress Cataloging-in-Publication Data

Heed, Peter
     Canoe racing : the competitor's guide to marathon and downriver canoe racing / Peter Heed & Dick Mansfield.
        p.   cm.
   Includes bibliographical references (p.) and index.
   ISBN 0-937921-52-1 : $14.95
        1. Canoe racing - - United States. 2. Canoe Racing, Marathon - - United States. I. Mansfield, Dick   II. Title.
   GV786.H42   1992
   797.1'4 - - dc20   92-3640
                                        CIP

Printed in the United States of America

1 2 3 4 5 6 7 8 9 10

Welcome to the world of marathon and downriver canoe racing and the first book on the subject in over a decade.

As the sport of canoe racing has grown, techniques have changed and equipment has become light and fast. At the same time, there has been an information gap. Nowhere could an entrant to the sport find, in one place, how to race marathon canoes. We have tried to fill that gap.

We have assumed that readers have a basic understanding of exercise and canoeing and thus have concentrated on the topics pertaining directly to the sport of canoe racing. We have provided a listing of reference books for more detailed information on specific subjects such as general canoe strokes, weight training, and whitewater terminology.

We have highlighted ideas of special interest with over fifty **Heed's Hints**, practical racer-to-racer tips which you will find in bold print interspersed throughout the book.

This is a book for paddlers of all abilities. We hope that you will find information that will not only help you become a better paddler but will also increase your enjoyment of the sport that we love.

We would like to thank the many individuals and organizations who helped with this project. Eric Evans, Bob MacDowell, Bill Gardner, Steve Galib, Bob Rapant, Betty Ketter, Frank Stasz, Dave Armstrong, and Tanna Fries were among many who provided technical advice. Cindy Gilligan provided invaluable aid in manuscript preparation. Priscilla Reinertsen, Mary Robb Mansfield, and Tricia Heed gave us practical and concise editorial review comments.

A project like this could not be done without the support and understanding of our spouses and families — Tricia, Travis, and Ethan Heed; Mary, Jennifer, Richard, and Robb Mansfield.

Peter Heed
Dick Mansfield

March 1992

Contents

Chapter 1

Confessions Of A Canoe Racer

"There is magic in the feel of a paddle and the movement of a canoe, a magic compounded of distance, adventure, solitude, and peace."
Sigurd Olson.

It is mid-March. There is still ice on most of the rivers in New England. The ice on the particular river we are paddling this day has gone out about a week ago, but the current is still filled with millions of tiny ice cubes. Just a few days ago I was in a cross-country ski race; now I find myself out with a bunch of crazed canoe racers paddling our kevlar hulls through what feels like a giant Slurpee. It is twenty-four degrees. My hands are cold, my feet are cold. Yet there are ten canoes out with us this Sunday morning, occupied by racers of all types and abilities.

What pulls us out of our snug homes on this bone-chilling day? Surely, some would prefer to be home still warm in bed or having a leisurely brunch with the family. What's wrong, after all, with catching a few games of basketball on the tube? Still, here we are, out on a cold river, each of us with hopes and dreams of perhaps becoming better than we were last year. We are all out participating in canoe sport and sharing the joy of making a canoe go fast.

Making a canoe go fast — that's a big part of what draws me to the water. For me, bringing a racing canoe up to speed, watching and sensing as it seems to dance across the water, is a special thrill.

I am fascinated by the connectedness between hull and water — so intense and immediate. Just a short single-bladed paddle to make the racer one with the water and to provide all the motive power. This is so unlike the sensation generated by the relatively giant oars of a rowing shell or the long double-bladed paddle of a kayak. It's part of the magic.

Photograph by Tricia Heed

Sleek racing canoes are "magic" to paddle.

A canoe and a paddle; a simple craft and a simple tool. Yet, as Sigurd Olson knew so well, there is indeed magic in the feel of a paddle and moving a canoe through the water. Even when sprinting a racing canoe at top speed, we are not making the boat go particularly fast in relative terms — seven or eight miles per hour at most. But within the confines of the canoe, it feels as if you are flying.

Courtesy of Dick Foster

C-1's at the 1988 Nationals "flying" off the starting line.

I have often reflected on the source of this feel of "magic" that comes from paddling a sleek racing canoe and have never been able to put my fingers precisely on it. Still, the magic is undeniably there, and it is one of the primary reasons that I became and remain a canoe racer. Since I've started, let me confess some of the other reasons I love to race canoes.

For people who have never had the opportunity of paddling a modern racing canoe, it may appear that I have baked my brain cells by paddling out under the hot sun too long. This is because most people's experience with canoeing has been limited to kneeling uncomfortably in a heavy recreational canoe of less-than-inspired design. "Bruisewaters" is what the late canoeing guru Harry Roberts liked to call them. Whatever you call them, they are not particularly fun to paddle. Unfortunately, too many of the recreational canoes you find in backyards are heavy, slow (read "inefficient"), and just plain dull to paddle. If you are looking for the magic, you will not find it here.

Instead, climb aboard a "racing canoe," which is really nothing more than a light, sleek, well-designed canoe with comfortable bucket seats. Grab yourself a lightweight bent shaft racing paddle and take a few strokes in this canoe. That's all it will take to start to feel the magic. You have just gone from work boots to running shoes; from a pickup truck to a Ferrari; from a plow horse to a thoroughbred. Just a few minutes in one of these racing hulls and you will know exactly what Sigurd Olson was talking about.

Another source of canoe magic is the historical origins of the craft itself. Paddle any canoe for any distance and you are partaking in one of the oldest transportation rituals on the North American Continent. The versatile canoe has undergone surprisingly few changes from the early Indian designs many hundreds of years ago. As Dave Harrison points out in his marvelous book *Canoeing Skills For The Serious Paddler*, "No other craft except possibly the Eskimo kayak, combines so well the elements of speed, maneuverability, lightness, and load carrying capacity." Because the canoe is so versatile its essential design has remained intact over the centuries. The similarities between J. Henry Rushton's designs of the late nineteenth century and those of our modern racing hulls are striking. It is clear that today's canoe racers are not the first to feel the magic.

Canoe racing is unique in all of the world of sport in that it provides endurance competitions where the focus is exclusively on the muscles of the arms and upper torso, together with the cardiovascular system. Think about it. What other endurance sport relies totally on the upper body for propulsion? The classic endurance sports such as running, biking, cross-country skiing, and triathlons combine cardiovascular endurance with muscular endurance of the lower body, especially the legs. And even though there is an upper body component in cross-country skiing and swimming, the heavy bulk of the propulsion chores is carried by the legs. Only in canoe racing is the musculature of the upper body stressed exclusively and totally for hours on end. This great sport is, in fact, the last haven for the non-running endurance athlete.

Photograph by Chris Wingender

Two of the world's fastest paddlers, Olympic Gold Medalist Greg Barton and Canadian ace, Serge Corbin, teamed up to win the 1989 Nationals.

This fact is vividly demonstrated by Greg Barton. Greg, who won two gold medals at the Olympics in Seoul, Korea, in singles and doubles kayak, became the first American to win an Olympic gold medal in either canoeing or kayaking for many many years. I first met Greg some time ago, long before his Olympic days. He was paddling marathon canoes at the time (and still races marathon canoes on occasion), and what struck me were his calf muscles.

They were obviously atrophied and he appeared to have some problems running. I later learned that Greg had suffered from a club foot-type birth defect. His lower legs were in stark contrast to the rest of his incredibly muscled body, yet he has obviously never allowed his problem to interfere in any way with his goals and determination to reach those goals. Not only did Greg go on to become one of the fastest paddlers in the world, he remains a modest and unselfish young man, so typical of the majority of people who participate in canoe racing.

No, you don't need great leg speed to be a successful canoe racer. In fact, except for long portages, running ability is just about irrelevant. Not the fastest kid on your block? Have a gimpy knee from an old football injury or too many miles on the road? This sport of canoe racing is for you.

Another feature of the magic of canoe racing is the fact that the sport is ideally suited for women — and vise-versa. In the early days of canoe racing, women participants were few and far between. Back then it was thought that women were not physically able to stand up to the rigors of marathon length events. Besides, you needed big strong arms for canoe racing. Right? Wrong!

Athletes like Grete Waitz and Joan Benoit Samuelson have demonstrated to us that women are physiologically well-suited for endurance events. In canoe racing, elite paddlers like Tanna Fries, Jan Whitaker, Roxanne Barton, and Bunny Johns can match all but a few top male paddlers. "Big arms" are not at all required for canoe racing. Instead, what you need is a strong torso and back, and a good cardiovascular system. Like any endurance sport, you also need determination, desire, and the discipline to train. And the last thing you need — the thing that makes women so wonderfully suited for marathon canoe racing— is a good strength-to-weight ratio. That's because canoe racers must paddle their canoes through the amount of water they displace. So while a 250-pound man with a powerful football lineman type body may be mighty strong in a muscular sense, because he will be displacing his weight in water when he sits in a canoe, his endurance is likely to wane quickly. On the other hand, a sinewy 110-pound female may be able to make that canoe get up and fly and keep it going for hours. While certain limitations in maximum oxygen uptake and other physiological features prevent women from competing on an equal basis with similarly talented and trained males, it's interesting to note that the top mixed teams in canoe races can beat or equal all but the very best men's teams. If you're a woman who enjoys endurance sports, canoe racing could be just what you are looking for.

Photograph by Chris Wingender

Lead Women's C-1 racers working upstream at the 1989 Nationals.

Another source of the magic in canoe racing for me is that injuries are so rare. While the term "low impact" is all the rage right now, even that description is too severe for canoe racing. Try "no impact." In canoe racing, your weight is totally supported by the canoe and you are really propelling your slender craft forward by locking your paddle blade into the water. To be sure, there are stresses to the muscles of the back and neck but you won't have jarring or impact type situations arise. In over twelve years of competitive paddling, I know of only a few racers who have received sufficient injury from paddling to require them to rest and recover for more than a week.

Canoe racing is also a relatively safe sport. With the exception of whitewater racing, the bodies of water on marathon race courses are placid, making self-rescue generally a safe and sure procedure. Yet canoe racing is not entirely without danger. There are cold water, fallen trees (strainers), dams, and power boaters to contend with. But you are not going to get run over by a car or a truck, nor are you going to come crashing to the pavement in a bike crash. As you'll see in the chapters that follow, almost all the serious dangers associated with canoe racing are easily avoided with an application of common sense and basic safety precautions.

With each passing year, I have come to appreciate another source of canoe racing's magic — the fact that the sport is so safe and so impact free that it is perfect for the mature athlete. Canoe racing's biggest growth in recent years has come in the Masters (ages 40 to 50), Seniors (ages 50 to 60), and Veterans (ages 60 and up) Classes. And, because canoeing is a weight-supported activity and does not generally stress the cardiovascular system quite to the extent that running or cross-country skiing does, you find that there is very little drop-off in performance levels until paddlers get well into their fifties. For example, the fastest C-1 men's time at the 1991 USCA National Championships was turned in by Michigan's Ken Kolonich — a masters paddler!

Gene Jensen, the famous canoe designer and racer who is now over 60 and who won the C-1 Veterans National Championship at the 1991 USCA Nationals, represented the attitude of most masters paddlers when I overheard him say, "I spent my first twenty years of canoe racing trying to prove I'm a man, and the next twenty years of canoe racing trying to prove I'm a boy."

Another important factor for me, and I think for most racing paddlers, is that the training experience can be so darn pleasant. No matter how many competitions you enter each season, the majority of your time will be spent training. There's simply no better way to relax and get alone with your thoughts than to be out in your canoe on some river or lake. It is a life-enhancing activity which provides you with the opportunity to be close to nature and experience the sensory pleasures of gliding through a liquid medium.

Have you ever seen how different and lovely the world can look from river level? When paddling hard in a pre-race workout, you can see blue herons, feeding deer, or a rising trout. Even when rivers and streams flow through residential and urban areas, the perspective from your canoe seat is so different that you normally feel isolated from the hectic day-to-day activities of our modern urban world. To me, canoe training is not only good for the body and the soul, it is aesthetically pleasing. No matter how rigorous my workout has been, I never fail to feel refreshed and vitalized when I step out of the canoe.

Courtesy of We-no-nah Canoe Company

Gene Jensen, with stern partner Dan Hassel in the 1973 International Classique in Quebec, is credited with most breakthroughs in modern marathon canoe design. He also introduced the bent shaft racing paddle.

Lastly, one of the most special aspects about the sport of canoe racing is the high level of commitment to good sportsmanship exhibited by nearly all competitors. This was one of the first lessons for me early on in my canoe racing experience. Competitors would come up to me after races and give me suggestions on how to improve my technique or my training. This certainly was not what I had grown used to in other competitive sports. But, canoe racing is, by and large, a self-coached sport and most of the best paddlers will tell you that they learned how to race with the help and guidance of other racers. This "helping your competitor" is one of the great traditions of the sport.

This tradition was dramatically reinforced for me during the 1991 General Clinton 70-miler. We were just a little more than a third of the way into the race, at about the three hour mark. My partner Paul Facteau and I were running with two other canoes, battling for for 7th, 8th, and 9th places. As we came into the Goodyear dam portage, I saw, too late, Paul throw away his drink jug. He thought we were being re-supplied at the end of the portage but in fact, we were not going to receive any more liquid until the next portage, at Oneonta, almost an hour down the course! Being without liquid for an hour at this point in a long race is often disastrous. I was sure that Paul would become dehydrated and we would have to drop out of the race.

After the portage, the teams paddling next to us became aware of the dire situation we were in. I expected that they would take this opportunity to put the hammer down and leave us to languish in our dehydrated state. But that's not what happened at all.

In an unselfish display of sportsmanship, Bob Wisse and Jeff Shultis, two New York pro canoe racers who were in our small pack, volunteered to help. Bob, who was in the bow, handed his drinking tube to my partner Paul who proceeded to suck down the much needed liquid. Watching it from the stern as we moved down the river, I was reminded of two jets refueling in flight. Bob and Jeff did this for us on several occasions down to Oneonta, and it literally saved our race. We were able to continue and eventually finish in 9th place — all thanks to one of our direct and closest competitors. (Wisse and Shultis did beat us, by one place. Poetic justice!)

As you've figured out by now, I confess that I'd rather be out paddling a racing canoe than just about anything else in the world. Cynics think that's because I'm not real good at anything else; others think that I just like to get away from the stresses and strains of job and everyday life. The truth is simple. Like Sigurd Olson, I feel the magic. You will too.

Chapter 2

Getting Started In Canoe Racing

"The race is my adventure."
Dr. George Sheehan

Several of us waited in the shallows of the Susquehanna River, cameras at the ready, for the racers to come up the river. They were nearly finished with the eighteen-mile race and only had this short stretch against the current before turning toward the finish line.

A group of "standard" canoes, which had started earlier, cruised by as we crouched in the August-warm water and clicked away. Led by a couple of young men, the first group looked strong and competent. Then, as the canoes kept coming, the paddlers were a little less accomplished, a little more tired, but still enjoying the beautiful day and knowing that they were almost home. Some smilingly asked for a push through the shallows, others preened momentarily as they went by saying such things as, "I hope you got my best side," a bald stern paddler yelled, "I can't do a thing with my hair." Seventy-one year-old Dr. John Ayer and his partner of the same age, Herm Schlimmer, cruised past, intent on passing some of their younger competitors, and doing it.

Then, looking downriver, we spotted four sets of paddlers snaking their way up the shoreline, carbon-fiber paddles flashing at a high turnover rate, using the eddies and the shallows to beat the

Photograph by Tricia Heed

Keeping the hammer down. It takes intensity and effort to stay in front.

current. It was an amazing sight, eight supremely-conditioned young men, "duking it out" stroke for stroke in less than two feet of water, drafting off each other, streaking toward the finish. They passed and soon, dozens in their competition class followed. Later still, recreational-minded paddlers passed, in many cases just paddling to finish, but always with a smile or a quip for the camera.

Yes, canoe races can be exciting spectator and competition events. Nowhere is this more evident than at the Classique Internationale de Canots where every year, thousands of spectators crowd the main street of Shawinigan, Quebec, to clap and yell for canoe racers. Cheering in French and English, they urge the teams of canoeists to run faster. This portage, where the racers lug their canoes on their shoulders through a narrow gap in the crowd, is infused with the carnival atmosphere that one finds during the climbs in the Tour de France or coming off the Queensboro Bridge in the New York marathon.

So, if you mix water, Kevlar, enthusiastic crowds, and well-

Courtesy of Le Nouvelliste

All top canoe racers love to run down the famous Boulevard portage, cheered by thousands, during the Classique Internationale de Canots.

trained athletes, you have a recipe for exciting competition. This charged atmosphere is found everywhere canoeists race: the Hudson River Whitewater Weekend in New York; the Kenduskeag River Race near Bangor, Maine; Michigan's Ausable Marathon; the Great Josh Billings Triathlon; or in hundreds of local races scattered across the United States and Canada.

Canoe racing is truly a sport for all ages and all levels of competence. While accomplished elite men and women, many of whom you might see at cycling or cross country ski races, vie for the top honors, in other classes, recreational canoes play bumper tag in some hair-raising starts and finishes. In most races, there are many paddlers who enter just to finish, for the fun, the camaraderie, and for a good workout.

Canoe racing can be as technical as aerodynamic theory, but it can also be as laid back as "Let's borrow Joe's canoe and get on a triathlon team." There's room in the sport for anyone who wants to give it a try. In this book, we'll tell you how to get into canoe racing or, if you're already hooked, how to improve your racing results. But, before we start calling "huts" and leading you through a shallow water sprint, let's take a look at what's going on in North American canoe racing today.

Photograph by Jim Mack

The future of the sport is reflected by these fledgling paddlers learning the joy of racing fast canoes.

Finding The Races

On any given weekend from March to November, there are dozens of canoe races taking place. Some, like New York's General Clinton, feature hundreds of canoes and involve everyone from pro racers to teams of Girl and Boy Scouts, each racing in a specific category. Other events are local in nature with several dozen racers, similar to a small 10 kilometer road race. Still other races involve stretches of whitewater or the run/bike/canoe triathlon sequence. Paddlers just getting started in canoe racing are often surprised at the number of races scheduled each season. The trick is to learn about them — it is sometimes difficult for newcomers to get hooked up with the canoe racing scene until they make some contacts and get on some mailing lists. Conversely, it is surprising, once you get started, to find so many races that have been occurring near you.

As in any sport, it helps to find someone who is active in the sport. Be inquisitive. If you see a racing canoe strapped on a parked

Photograph by Michelle Lavigne

Thrills and spills go along with downriver racing.

Courtesy of Athol Daily News

Each spring the Athol, Mass. "Rat Race" draws hundreds of paddlers of all abilities.

vehicle, ask the owner if he or she races and how you can pick up more information. Visit a local canoe race and talk to racers after the event. You'll find that canoeists are proselytes at heart — they are more than willing to welcome you to their sport and are always looking for converts. Be a joiner. Pick the canoe racing group closest to you and join it. In many parts of the country, groups of canoe racers get together, often on a mid-week evening, and train together. It's a great place to pick up information and advice. You also should join the two major canoe organizations, the U. S. Canoe Association and the American Canoe Association. You'll get each group's publication, race schedules, and often be placed on mailing lists for race announcements.

Most regional canoe clubs not only list upcoming races, they also conduct clinics where new paddlers get a chance to learn more about handling a canoe. Some groups will have organized time trials or training outings — it is a great place to pick the brains of more experienced racers. (See Resource Section for major clubs.)

Types of Races

There are two main categories of long distance canoe racing: marathon canoe races and downriver races. Marathon canoe races encompass everything from a local Rotary-sponsored race to professional events lasting several days. They vary in length from about 5 miles to over 100 miles and average in the 7-15 mile range. The water is normally calm and often there will be a portage or two. There are many classes for competitors. Larger races start by class; smaller races often have a mass start.

Downriver races are whitewater distance races that are nearly as long as some marathon races. Canoes are normally started individually, one every minute or so. There are many classes in downriver racing including classes specifically for the recreational paddler in his or her "backyard" ABS canoe.

Courtesy of Le Nouvelliste

There are many rewards from canoe racing.

There are other types of canoe races that will not be covered in this book in any detail. These include flat water sprint canoe racing (Olympic events), whitewater slalom and wildwater (closed canoes), dragon boat racing, and outrigger events. Kayak racing is also not included. Our focus is on open canoe marathon, downriver, and triathlon events.

Types of Classes

Canoe racing has evolved, like most other participation sports, into a relatively standard series of race classes which are based on the age and sex of the paddlers as well as the type of canoe being used. Masters classes generally start at age 40, Seniors at age 50, and Veterans at age 60. Juniors are racers under age 19.

Here is a breakdown of classes used in one large race:

C-2 Men	C-2 Men Masters
C-2 Women	C-2 Mixed
C-2 Jr./Sr.	C-2 Pro Boats (3 x 27)
C-2 Junior	C-2 Family Racing
C-1 Men	C-1 Masters
C-1 Seniors/Veterans	C-1 Women
C-2 Recreational (& Masters)	
C-2 Family (Recreational)	C-2 Standard

Whether you are a high-schooler or a grandparent, there is probably a class for you in canoe racing. While not all races have as many classes as shown above, most make up as many as possible so that like-aged people are racing against one another in similar types of boats.

Canoe racing is fun. Whether you plan to launch your neighbor's Grumman for the first time in a recreation class, or to train hard for months before the season and compete against the best, the satisfaction of being on the water, racing against paddlers similarly equipped, is a great experience. You will find, regardless of your expertise, that canoe racing is quite a thinking person's sport. As you learn to paddle more efficiently, to use the energy of the wakes of others, to read the river, and to pace yourself and your partner, you find that one need not be an Arnold Schwarzenegger to make a canoe go fast. Read on and you'll learn how to get going and get faster. Throw your life jacket in the boat and we're off.

Chapter 3

Equipment

Tools Of The Canoe Racing Trade

"Few things invented by the human mind come so close to perfection as a well-made canoe."

Ben Bachman

People get hooked on canoe racing for a variety of reasons. Perhaps you are a recreational paddler planning to enter a local race. Or you are going to sign up for a team triathlon, borrow an old fiberglass canoe, practice for a few days, and on race day, go out and thrash away along with several dozen paddlers in a hot race. As you get to thinking about buying a racing canoe — and you will — there are many factors that need to be considered before stepping out and laying down the cash for a racing boat. What sort of canoe do you think you want? One person, two person, wood strip, or Kevlar? Will you rent, borrow, buy used, or buy new?

We have some ideas about how to go about getting the best equipment that fits you, your budget, and your racing goals. Here's how to become a smart canoe consumer.

Buying a Canoe (or two, or three!)

Canoe design has come a long way from the canvas-covered craft of the "Paddlin' Madeline Home" era. There are now hundreds of wood strip, fiberglass, Kevlar, and carbon fiber models available to fit any pocketbook. As racing designs get slicker, lighter, stiffer, and more expensive, there are many used racing boats out there for the discriminating shopper. Most of these used racing hulls are as fast, or close to it, as the more expensive canoes that their former owners upgraded to. That's the good news.

When starting out, consider buying a good used boat. You are bound to bang up any canoe when you get started so why not pick one up that's already scratched. You can always sell it or keep it as a training boat later on.

The bad news is this: when you try to sort out which of these wonderful craft will be the perfect canoe for your needs and resources, the choice is mind-boggling. But there's hope. What you need to do is to stick with some basics. In this chapter, we'll concentrate on canoes that are best used for the different classes of marathon racing in relatively gentle water. (Downriver canoes, as noted in Chapter 11, are a somewhat different design.)

Photograph by Dick Mansfield

The choice of a racing canoe can be mind-boggling.

To get started, answer these three questions:

Do I want to paddle alone or with a partner?
What are my racing objectives?
How much money am I ready to spend?

These are questions that every newcomer should consider. And, interestingly enough, they are the questions that seasoned racers face when their situations change: for example, they get married and want to have their spouse as a partner, or they decide to concentrate more on C-1 racing. It is not easy, until you begin racing and develop some knowledge of the sport, to come up with good answers. So, do some homework. Talk to racers, take a dealer's demo boat for a paddle, borrow an old canoe, borrow a new canoe. But before we get much further, the envelope please. What was your answer to question 1? (*Do I want to paddle alone or with a partner?*)

Tandem Canoe Racing

Most marathon canoe racers "do their thing" in a two-seated canoe commonly known as a C-2. It's a great way to race — you can have fun working together as a fluid team and, with a little practice, can really make that boat move. There are many advantages to racing with a partner: you have someone to learn, blame, splash, laugh with; someone to encourage you, to share successes and failures with; someone to help handle the canoe in tricky water or rough going. It allows all sorts of combinations: man and man, man and woman, woman and woman, or parent and child to team up and race together.

Another real advantage of tandem or "doubles" canoeing is cost — beginners can get a lot of boat for their money. First of all, if you want to start off in recreational classes, you can always use the family canoe and get a great workout. It won't be long before you get frustrated and want to get your hands on a true racing canoe. Even in the advanced racing classes, there are a lot of used C-2's available as owners have upgraded to newer designs and materials.

You can buy a good used C-2 for $500-$700. If you split that cost with a partner, it gets you into canoe racing quite reasonably.

But there are downsides, as many solo canoeists, who began with a partner or two, have found. Every racing season, about July, if you hang out at races you'll hear, "Next year I'm getting a C-1. I'm not getting enough training in because John (or Jan) is often not available to train when I can."

Courtesy of Norwich Bulletin

Some husband/wife teams, such as Herm and Sue Botzow, shown passing a men's recreational team on the Patchogue River, have raced together for many years.

Finding a compatible racing partner is no easy trick. Canoe racing requires teams to train together in the boat, to show up on time for practices and for races, to be able to work together. Not all people have identical goals for training and competition — you may only want to jump into a few races a year and leave the weekends free for other activities while your partner may want to train every night and race every weekend. And even if you have the same training and racing goals, sometimes you just can't get two schedules to allow consistent practice.

On the other hand, there are many sets of long-term partners in canoe racing and some good wife/husband teams who have paddled together for years. If you buy a C-2 or share in the ownership of one, be realistic about the fact that things will change down the road. It's not a problem. There are many good paddlers around — if you know what you are doing and find it fun to work with another paddler, you won't have trouble finding a C-2 partner.

Solo Canoe Racing

Solo canoes are increasingly the choice of many newcomers to canoe racing who are looking at the sport as a training and racing alternative. Many are runners, skiers, and cyclists who are planning to do canoe triathlons on their own or who are interested in cross-training. Many canoe racers who are primarily C-2 racers have a solo boat to practice in for the days when they can't get together with their C-2 partner. (Many canoe race weekends have C-1 races on one day and C-2 the other, so these folks can race both canoes.)

> **The big advantage of a C-1 canoe is that it is available when you are. There's no need to see if "partner" wants to go — you just load up and do it. It's a no-hassle way to get some on-the-water training in on short notice. Nothing beats the convenience of a C-1, ready to go on the roof rack.**

C-1 canoes do have some drawbacks. They usually require a higher degree of skill to handle. Some can be pretty "squirrelly" for novice paddlers — I took several unplanned swims during my first season of C-1 paddling. Tandem boats, with two paddles available for stability, tend to be less tippy.

For some, a major problem with solo paddling is boredom. You often will be paddling along, working on technique, all by your lonesome. The "loneliness of the long distance paddler" can get to you. Some paddlers like this solitude; others compare it to an exercise bike or rowing machine — 30 minutes is enough. Dennis Williams, who has won many canoe ironman competitions, says, "In long canoe races, when we were really split up, I'd sometimes slow up, just to let a boat catch me so that it would break the boredom." In training, C-1 paddlers can make plans to paddle side by side, working on drafting and having a chance to chat.

> **Try to break the C-1 boredom with music. I often take a Walkman and a tape of "psych music" along on my C-1 outings on the Connecticut River and work on technique during the first half of the session. Then I put the earphones on and paddle back to music.**

There are more and more used C-1 canoes available — usually all-out racing canoes. There have been major design changes in the last eight years so be careful about buying a solo boat that is obsolete. You may find older boats too heavy and slow — and end up buying a newer version after only a season of paddling.

Racing Objectives
How did you answer? *What are my racing objectives?*

Serious Competitor
What sort of a canoe racer will you be? Are you a person who is very competitive and runs, cycles, or skis near the front of the pack? A Type A personality? Obviously, you want the fastest boat that you can buy — which means a late model used canoe or one right out of the shop. Don't be concerned about handling the boat. That will come. It's just like skiing on racing skis — what you trade for a little stability is more than made up for in speed and fun.

Check out what the lead pack racers are using for equipment. Ask them, after a race, if you can take their boat for a little paddle.

Racers are the same from sport to sport. They love to share information with newcomers. When you check out the fast boats, be cautious about unproven models, especially from little-known manufacturers. Let someone else be the test driver. Look at competition cruisers in the C-2 category or a new C-1 and be ready to part with $1200 to $2000 for a new racing canoe; somewhat less for a late-model used racing canoe. Concentrate on Kevlar or carbon-fiber canoes — fiberglass is too heavy for top-drawer competition. Be sure to check out the light-weight woodstrip canoes. They are more fragile but are stiff and fast — and beautiful.

Photograph by Dick Mansfield

A new racing canoe will cost $1200 to $2000.

In-Touch-With-Reality Paddlers

You say you've got three kids in college. Or you work long hours and can't train the way you'd like to. Or you are old enough to have paddled canvas canoes. For the not-so-serious competitor, there are lots of options available in racing canoes. We recommend that you look hard at some of the older Kevlar craft, the fiberglass boats, and the older stripper boats. Go to some races and notice how many canoes are for sale. Again, stick with the proven models and talk to the best paddlers. Many trade up for new canoes each year and will cut a fair deal on their older boats. Wouldn't it be fun to buy a boat that was trained to go fast!

Have Fun With A Friend Paddler

Early one morning, I met two paddlers in a nice looking Kevlar C-2 who were sitting on a pier, getting ready to paddle. In talking with them, I learned that they enter only one race a year, the popular Great Race triathlon in Auburn, New York. "We're not good enough to get in other races," they said, "and besides, it's too much work to get in shape." But here they were, 6:30 in the morning, practicing for a four-mile race a month away. That's all the canoe racing they were interested in and the boat that they had was more than adequate for them.

There is an important point here — if you are unsure of how often or how seriously you'll be racing, still try to get as much boat as you can afford. Go for a new or used USCA cruiser, or a less racy option, a standard class canoe. Standard class is a good place for many to begin — or change their mind about — their racing careers. These canoes, with their more conservative design, are more for-giving than competition cruisers, yet they are light and swift enough to be fun. Plan to pay between $600 to $800 for an older model and more for a new one.

Recreational Paddlers

You don't want, or can't afford, one of those *racing* canoes. As we have said before, you can race the family canoe in almost any canoe race. As you'll see throughout this book, hundreds of aluminum and ABS canoes race against one another all over the country. It is a cheap way to get into racing and find out if you want to spring for a faster boat. These canoes are slow but functional — you can cruise, fish, or even race rapids with them. Plan to pay $400 to $900 for a decent recreational hull.

Photograph by Dick Mansfield

There are recreation classes in most marathon and downriver races.

Types Of Racing Canoes

Newcomers to canoe racing should have an understanding of canoe categories. (The United States Canoe Association sets the specifications for marathon racing except in the recreational class.) At most large canoe races, there are about five or six major categories of canoes. These are:

Recreational — A loosely defined class that includes most backyard canoes and general purpose boats.

Aluminum — Stock aluminum boats (Grummans & Alumacrafts, for example) which can be up to 18 1/2 feet in length. Still a large class in parts of the U.S., however, the concept of defining a class by the material is one whose time is past.

Standard — A semi-recreational class boat. These fairly sleek hulls are almost as fast as a cruiser but are a bit wider and more stable. They are a good all-around choice for novice racers with limited aspirations. Standards have a maximum length of 18' 6" and must widen to at least 15% of the length at the 4 inch waterline.

<u>Competition Cruiser</u> — The main amateur racing canoe. Designed for speed, they feature swept-in bows and sterns and limited freeboard. They have a maximum length of 18' 6" and the width-to-length ratio at the 4 inch waterline is 14.375%. This translates into a canoe which measures 32" at the widest point. Hence, these hulls are also know as 4 x 32 boats. There are different cruisers for mixed teams and similar-weight teams, so make sure you know what you're looking for. USCA cruisers make up the largest class in most marathons and triathlons. If you really want to get into racing, get one of these boats.

<u>3 x 27 "Pro Boats"</u> — Similar to a cruiser in outward appearance, this design has even less freeboard and more radical hull design. You can easily tell them by the covered decks and the advertising on the sides, all of which is permitted in this class. These canoes also max out at 18' 6" and must be a minimum 27" wide at a point on the 3" waterline. These hulls are used in most professional races and are the predominant design in Canada, Michigan, and several western states.

<u>C-1</u> — Solo marathon cruisers come in lengths up to 18' 6" and are swept in at the bow and stern with a wide "wing" section in the middle. They generally follow the same specifications as the USCA cruisers. Most are made of Kevlar, wood strip, or carbon/Spectra. This is the fastest growing class in marathon canoe racing today.

Photograph by Peter Heed

Note the marked design difference between the racing cruiser on the left and a general recreational canoe.

Photographs by Peter Heed

From left to right: a downriver racer, a USCA competition cruiser, a 3X27 "pro" boat, and a C-1 marathon racer.

Canoe Buying Hints

You need a boat tailored to your physique and your racing plans — a light two-woman team may want to pick a different boat from a duo where one partner outweighs the other by 50 pounds or more. Likewise, a 195-pound paddler will be best suited for a longer and wider C-1 than a smaller, shorter paddler.

Talk to knowledgeable dealers and distributors — tell them your plans and see what they suggest. Do the same with experienced paddlers. Pick their brains. Look over the canoes at races; check workmanship, notice how they are set up. If you are near a shop with a selection of canoes, inspect a few. Look for flaws, little pools of resin, humps or dips in the bottom, and overall quality. Check used boats for cracks, serious gouges, delaminated wooden gunwales, and evidence of abuse. Stick with known models — let someone else check out the merits of a newly-minted design.

What you will find, if you are buying new, is that few dealers have many canoes in inventory. But don't let that bother you. Most of the racing canoes bought each year are ordered sight unseen. That's where a known dealer and supplier comes in — there shouldn't be any surprises when the canoe shows up. In some respects, buying a used canoe is easier because you can inspect it, paddle it, and probably even haggle about price. Take a knowledge-able paddler with you to look at used canoes. You want to avoid not only major flaws but also those designs that never quite made it.

As you might expect, the best time to buy a canoe is in the fall, just near the end of the racing season. Go to a local race — you will find "For Sale" signs on a number of canoes as owners plan for the winter and year ahead. Also, be sure to check club newsletters which always have a handy "For Sale" page.

Buying a Paddle

Paddle design and construction evolved into a high tech form in the 1980's. Now, nearly all canoe racers use carbon fiber paddles of bent shaft design. (The bent shaft, first introduced by canoe design guru Gene Jensen, allows the blade to be vertical in the water for more of the stroke, thus delivering more usable thrust.) Bent shafts are lighter and easier to handle. Paddle angles vary widely between 10° and 15°. Most racers use one between 12° and 14°. Any good paddle within that range will be just fine for beginning racers.

There are a wide variety of paddle grips available. More and more marathon paddlers favor a palm grip because it helps you to drive downward during the power phase. A T-grip gives more control over the blade and thus is favored by whitewater racers.

Paddle widths are getting narrower in marathon racing. Not long ago, paddles had blades that were 12-13 inches wide, the so-called "banjo paddles." The standard paddle width today is 8 to 8.5 inches for marathon racing.

About 80% of the paddlers can use a 50 to 52 inch paddle. Taller, lankier guys need a longer one. C-1 paddlers also need a longer paddle, generally, an inch or two longer than for a C-2, because you sit in the widest part of the canoe and therefore are farther away from the water, and have to do more things with the paddle. (If you paddle a 50 in C-2, you may want a 51 for C-1.) If a race has a lot of shallow water, a shorter paddle (about an inch) may be warranted.

In general, beginning canoe racers tend to use too long a paddle. You are trying to keep your upper hand in the power phase of the stroke at about eye level or below. When you are getting started, borrow a 50 to 52 paddle and give it a try, then go shorter or longer if needed.

A paddle is the place to splurge when you are picking up equipment. When I was considering my first paddle, Roberta Shapiro, an nationally-ranked paddler, advised me to start right out with a new carbon fiber paddle. "When you are new to the sport," she said, "you need all the help you can get. Why penalize yourself with a heavy paddle? Everyone you will be racing will have the black ones." I followed her advice and haven't regretted it. And she's right, nearly all racers now use composite paddles.

Good carbon fiber paddles cost from $140 to $190 but seven miles into a fourteen-mile race, you'll be glad you bought one. There are also many light-weight wood and composite bent shaft paddles that will fit the bill, especially in recreational racing, that cost between $75 and $100. Some paddlers start with one and later, upgrade to a carbon fiber and use the wooden paddle for a spare.

Plan to buy new. There are few used paddles around since most racers keep their old ones for spares. A good paddle is a big investment but like all quality gear, you get what you pay for. Why not put a carbon fiber paddle on your wish list for your birthday?

Clothing — Warm Weather

Canoe racing requires little in the way of new wardrobe. Men often race in running shorts and a pair of running shoes. Women often wear a singlet and biking shorts.

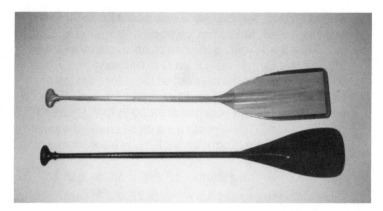

Photograph by Dick Mansfield

An older-style wooden paddle and a new carbon fiber paddle.

Get a personal flotation device (PFD) and if you are not a strong swimmer, wear it. You will want something light-weight and sized to fit. But even if, like most racers, you're simply going to stuff the life vest under the seat and use it only in an emergency, you still need a PFD that fits properly. Plan to spend about $50-$60 for a good PFD.

The special water shoes worn by wind surfers and others are perfect for most canoe racing. If there's a portage, light running shoes should be worn. (They also provide more stability against the foot brace.) An old pair of sneakers does nicely. Expert paddler Priscilla Reinertsen affectionately calls hers "my river shoes" and says, " You can tie them up to the thwart of your canoe after you have put the boat back up on your car. By the time you return home, your river shoes will be dry."

Be sure to protect your skin when paddling. Don't be fooled by breezes and relative coolness from the water: sun exposure can be very high. Sunscreens and hats are important. Racers like a hat that they can dip in the water to cool their head. A light colored T-shirt or singlet is often used with the Lycra triathlon shorts or running shorts. Don't forget to include a good pair of sunglasses which block ultraviolet light.

Clothing — Cold Weather

It is awkward to wear a wet suit when marathon paddling — most restrict your paddling and you tend to build up a lot of body heat quickly. Yet when it's very cold, you should consider one, especially if you are a novice and unsteady in the canoe. (You also might consider waiting a few weeks and getting in shape by safer means.) If you live in the snow belt and plan to paddle in early spring, plan to spend about $100 for a light-weight "Farmer John" type wet suit.

> **Cold weather paddling can be dangerous, particularly for a novice. I'm never more than 20-25 feet from shore when I paddle in early season. Try to go out with a group. There's safety in numbers.**

A better bet for most paddlers in cold weather is to layer with polypropylene and wool. (Wool retains a large proportion of its insulating value after getting wet.) Wool biking pants and a wool biking shirt over polypro provide you with a small but significant margin of safety after taking a dunk in cold water. This clothing also enables you to retain some heat once on shore.

Often in a training run in early spring, you'll start shedding your hat, gloves, and outerwear as you heat up. Make sure that you have some sort of dry bag with you so that you can stow the gear and have it ready as soon as you finish the session.

Gloves are needed in cold weather but since you're going to get your hands wet, many fine skiing and biking gloves are useless. One of the best solutions is a pair of thin wool gloves — they will tend to stay warm even when they are wet.

> **In real winter-type weather, I take a complete change of clothes — wool pants and shirt, gloves, and hat — and put them in a water-tight tote bag which I lock on a thwart. I leave the bag in the van so that it's ready the next trip. It's saved me several times — I get to the bank, strip and get on the dry clothes fast. When it was 35°, it felt great! Besides, you may give some poor startled onlooker a good thrill!**

Setting up the boat

So you've got a racing boat and new paddle. What now, coach? There are about as many ways to set up a canoe as there are racers — some paddlers are masters at it. When you go to the races, peer into boats, check out their drinking system, notice how the extra paddle is stowed, how the seat is adjusted. And as you get started, pick up some contact cement, some rigid foam (used for bottle holders, spray rails and paddle holders), as well as some thin ethafoam, such as that used for backpacking sleeping pads (for cushioning the gunnels and padding the seats.) You can find these materials at hardware and outdoor stores, and they also can be purchased from vendors at many canoe races.

Adjusting The Seat

For beginners, the most important step in getting the boat ready to use is to <u>lower the seat</u>. The higher the seat, the more unsteady the boat will be. It is amazing what a difference in stability lowering the seat a half inch or inch makes. Racing C-1's are pretty "squirrelly" and C-2's, while a little more stable, especially if you have a seasoned partner, also can be unsettling to the novice. It is hard to concentrate on paddling if you are continually worrying about going over. Lower the seat — you can always raise it later. What you might lose in leverage you more than make up in confidence.

> **Get to feel "at home" in a racing hull. Too many beginners just hop In the canoe and head right out the first time. Find a calm area, where it's not very deep, and get in the boat and play. Lean it, twirl it, go in circles, dump it. Lose the fear of falling out. When you are getting started in racing, almost every workout should include a little "rock and roll."**

You can usually lower the seat enough by simply hanging the seat under the supporting brackets. This small change will do wonders for your stability and confidence. Beginners and even more experienced racers should also try raising the back of the seat — or lowering the front. You want to cant the seat so that you are not sitting dead flat in the boat. Just getting the back of the seat a little higher sets you up better for the paddling motion and takes pressure off the nerves running down your leg. You also will be able to push more against the seat and feel more a part of the canoe. You can change most seats by simply getting longer bolts for the rear and putting in some sort of shim to raise the back about an inch. <u>We think that this is one of the most important adjustments most canoe racers can make to their boats.</u>

Besides canting the seat, you'll want to pad it, not just for cushioning, but to prevent your buttocks from sliding. Look at some racing canoes, you'll find a padding setup to fit every physique. Start with a flat layer of foam — the kind used for sleeping pads — and tailor the setup to fit your preference. Some paddlers like two or three layers; other cut holes in the pad where the pelvic bone hits. You have to experiment.

Always carry a roll of duct tape with your canoe gear. You can use it to form spray shields on the bow, tape race numbers to the boat, secure drink bottles to a thwart, or even do emergency repairs to punctures in the hull. Duct tape is the racer's Swiss Army Knife.

Photograph by Peter Heed

Bow setup. Note the spacers to raise the back of the seat rails. Also note the seat padding and the foam on the inside of gunnel.

Trimming The Boat

A trimmed canoe is a fast canoe. The importance of keeping a racing canoe running level cannot be overemphasized. If you are stern heavy, your speed will suffer dramatically. On the other hand, being bow heavy will not bother your speed but may cause the canoe to veer off line, making steering difficult.

To make things a bit more complicated, a canoe that is level and trim to start with won't stay that way at race speeds! Without getting into advanced hydronamic theory, suffice it to say that a canoe's stern will sink slightly once the canoe is underway. To counter this, you trim the canoe slightly bow down (1/2 to 1 inch) when it is at rest.

You trim a racing canoe by moving the seats forward or aft. In order to trim the canoe, you have to know when it is level. The simplest way to do that is to mark lines on the side of the boat. Put the empty canoe in calm water and mark a line on the bow and the stern an equal distance up, say an inch, from the water line. Then hop in the boat and have someone look at the boat and coach you. We recommend that new racers adjust their seats (or seat in a C-1) so that the canoe is a half-inch to one inch lower in the bow while stationary in the water.

Another common way to check trim is to throw water into the boat. This method can be a little sophisticated so we don't recommend it for beginners. The advantages are that you can do it yourself and once you learn, you can do it while moving. The water in the canoe should go gradually to the bow while you are sitting still. As soon as you start paddling, the water will come back due to the motion of the boat. If you are trimmed right and are stable in cruise, the water should stay in the center or slightly forward.

You will need a moveable clamp on your seat rail that can be easily adjusted so that you can lock it but also easily loosen it when needed. This allows you to move your seat and adjust the trim during a race or training session. While canoes usually come with a locked pin arrangement, nearly all racers prefer a clamp that can be adjusted with a quick twist. When at canoe races, you'll often see equipment vendors who sell such clamps at a nominal cost.

Trim is adjusted according to the race course. The more shallow the course, the more bow down you want to begin — if you are going to be in constant shallow water, it wouldn't hurt to be an inch and a half bow down. On a totally deep water course, a half-inch bow down would be plenty.

Foot Braces

Next to a properly adjusted seat, there is no more important item within the canoe than the foot brace. Both paddlers need to be well braced in the canoe to properly transfer paddle energy to forward boat movement.

Once you know where the seat should be for trim, you then adjust your foot brace. How far away you want it is strictly personal preference, but you should have your legs bent slightly.

Metal bar foot braces are used by the stern paddler in a C-2 and solo paddler in C-1. Foot loops, made of cloth strapping or cord, are attached to the metal foot brace to lock in the feet. You need to be able to lock into the boat so that when you roll the boat for a turn, you can hold the boat on the lean. A C-1 paddler uses the foot loops to rock the canoe to remove weeds from the bow.

The bow paddler in a C-2 does not require foot loops as his/her legs and feet are pretty well wedged into the confines of the narrow bow. However, most bow paddlers prefer a bow foot brace to push against. Such a brace is usually carved out of stiff foam which fits snugly within the bow without pushing out the sides of the boat. Other paddlers build a cross brace and fiberglass it right into the boat. In that case, you put the built-in foot brace as far forward as you would ever conceivably go and then pad back off that, giving the bow a nice rigidity. Pad the side of the gunnel with soft foam for a softer surface to place your legs against.

Bow paddlers soon learn that due to the shape of the bow, often their feet can not be placed side by side. You can usually get the heels together but end up putting the ball of one foot on top the other. It's not too comfortable so it helps to alternate feet. Some bow paddlers place a leg back under the seat while the other leg pushes against the brace and then alternate legs as comfort dictates.

Photograph by Peter Heed

A rear setup showing foot straps, bailer, and jug holder.

Bow paddlers can take a pair of old running shoes and shave the sides of the soles so that they fit better in the bow. A good pair of custom fit "bow shoes" is a valued commodity on the race circuit.

Drinking Systems

Dehydration is a major risk in canoe racing because of the duration of the races. You need to rig up a "hands-free" drinking system. Most canoe racers use a plain insulated jug, available for under $5 at a hardware store, and either tape it to a thwart or anchor it to the canoe with a stiff foam holder. You'll see dozens of such setups at any race.

Plastic surgical tubing is stuck down into the jug and usually looped up to the paddler by a Velco tab on a strap around the neck. Others attach the tube to the boat with Velcro and go to it when needed. Explore ways that will work for you so that you have liquid available throughout the race.

Bailers

We recommend that you have at least one bailer in the canoe —
a stern bailer in a C-2 and a center one in a solo boat. Bailers use a
venturi action to suck water out of the boat when it is moving. Just
push the bailer down and let the water drain out. Pull it up to close.
Bailers also can drain a boat during portages.

Try to buy a boat with a bailer, but if yours does not have one,
it is not hard to install one. Ask around and find someone who has
done it — few of us have the nerve to cut into a Kevlar boat on our
own. If you face rough deep water in a race, a bow bailer is
recommended as well.

Spare paddles

A spare paddle is a must. You can break a paddle on a rock, a
log, or on the bow of someone's boat — or sometimes a paddle will
crack for no apparent reason. Paddles can be just placed loose in the
canoe if there are no portages; however, it is better to attach them
securely with rigid foam holders or clamps.

> **Carry a spare paddle and you probably won't need
> it. Anchor it to the canoe with an ethafoam holder or
> "broom type" clamp. Be sure that you can get to it in
> a hurry.**

Watch

We recommend attaching a watch to a gunnel or a seat support
so that you can keep track of the time during races and training
sessions. This is particularly important during interval work when
you must keep a constant eye on the clock. A little duct tape will do
fine to secure the watch although some racers use more elaborate
Velcro setups.

Food Holders

In long races, you will need to take on food at "pit stops". Some
racers just leave the food in open plastic bags on the floor of the
canoe, but a little water in the boat can quickly wash away your

lunch. We recommend attaching plastic containers to the gunnels or gluing foam food holders to the bottom of the boat. This will keep your food organized and dry, and you will know where to find it when you need it.

Successful canoe racing is a combination of training, ability, tactics, and equipment. As in other skill sports, light-weight gear is not only fast, it is fun to use. There's a real thrill to getting a quick, light canoe moving fast through the water. So, decide whether you're going to paddle solo or with a partner, whether you are going to start as a hard-core racer or a casual competitor, and see what the bank account can bear. Then go out and buy the best boat and paddle that you can afford. You won't regret it.

Chapter 4

Technique
The Good, The Bad, And The Ugly

*"Building good technique requires accurate repetition of
the correct skill—it is impossible to overemphasize the basics."*
Eric Evans

Sooner or later, you will be in a canoe race and be side by side with another team of canoeists who look no stronger than you and your partner. And you are matching them stroke for stroke. Yet, little by little (or sometimes more suddenly), they just seem to pull away from your boat. What's going on here? What are they doing with those black blades that you're not doing? Why is their boat going faster?

Getting Started
Let's start by reviewing a few basics that you should know :
1. You should adjust the seats to distribute weight so that the canoe is trim. (See Chapter 3 for details.)
2. The larger, more powerful paddler usually is in the bow.
3. Partners paddle on opposite sides, switching every 6-10 strokes.
4. The bow paddler normally sets the pace.
5. The stern paddler usually calls the switches.

In this chapter, we are going to give you some advice to help you paddle better. We aren't going to get too technical — it's easy to go overboard (pardon the pun) in describing the subtleties of paddling technique. What we are going to do is to tell you how the best canoeists in the world use their paddles. We will also suggest that you get some coaching from a good canoeist and that you watch several videos. Then, as they say about getting to Carnegie Hall, it's just a matter of practice, practice, practice.

The Forward Stroke

Marathon racing canoes are designed to go straight and designed to go fast. The stroke that makes them move so fast is called the *forward stroke*. It is simple in concept but complex in execution — a classic case of "easier said than done."

You should keep in mind that there is no one perfect or correct paddling technique. Serge Corbin, Bruce Barton, Calvin Hassel, and Al Rudquist are all incredibly fast in a canoe but their stroke techniques all vary to some degree. However, there are some basic characteristics which they all share. These are the crucial elements in the forward stroke, and it is on these components that we will focus. They are: the catch, the power phase, and the recovery.

The Catch

Getting the paddle in the water and anchoring it is called the *catch*. This is, without argument, the most critical step in the forward stroke. This is where most paddlers make mistakes, where novices really lose power in their stroke.

To begin, get a firm mental picture of what you <u>are</u> doing and <u>not</u> doing. You are not trying to pull your paddle back through the water; you are trying to pull your canoe past your paddle. Your paddle blade is the mechanism for locking your paddle into the water, so you can use the major muscles of the back, arms, and torso to pull the canoe forward. As Mike Fries explains so well, your paddle is an anchor — so anchor it!

To get the paddle in the water, reach forward with the lower arm and drop your shoulder as you start the stroke. You should be sitting nearly erect with a slight forward lean. The shoulder of your lower arm should fold forward and down. Do not lunge forward or bend at the waist. As you reach forward, extend the lower arm, but don't lock it.

Simultaneously, reach up and across with the upper arm, so that the upper hand is directly over the paddle blade — effectively keeping the paddle perpendicular to the water. Bend or flex the upper arm slightly, keeping the elbow high and the forearm parallel to the water surface.

Courtesy of Dick Foster

Bow paddler Mike Fries shows a "picture perfect" catch.

A common mistake is to not reach far enough ahead when starting the stroke. Remember: the power is in front of you. Another tendency of beginners is to lunge forward, getting the boat bobbing up and down as it moves ahead.

There are a number of ways to get the paddle in the water. One is a straight down plant or stab. Many Canadian and western paddlers favor this method. Another method is a "D" stoke where you slice the blade in from the side. Lastly, there is a combination of the two — a half-stab, half-slice method. You have to find out what works for you. We recommend that beginners use the slice technique because it forces you to wait until you have the paddle blade buried before you pull.

Right at the beginning of the stroke, you must bury the whole blade in the water. You want as little air as possible, both in front and behind the blade. This will help anchor the paddle in the water, allowing you to pull the canoe forward. Remember, every inch your blade moves backward through the water is energy which is lost and <u>not</u> being applied to move the canoe ahead.

Postition just before the catch

Besides reaching too far forward, another often-made error is to start applying power to the paddle before you get the entire blade in the water. By and large, most people get the whole blade in the water by the <u>end</u> of the stroke, not the beginning. Not good! Let's pretend for a moment that we have a video camera underwater. A pro's paddle blade would be vertical in the water, moving smoothly without any burble, parallel with the keel line of the boat. On the other hand, a novice's paddle would start moving before it really got all the way into the water, so there would be cavitation (trapped air and disturbed water) around it. Also, it would most likely travel downward as it moved rearward and stay in the water well past the vertical. The result is blade slippage and a loss of forward motion.

You want to run a quiet boat. You want a smooth running boat. Every time the boat wiggles left or right or bobs up and down, you lose a little. This can play havoc with your speed and efficiency in a long race. Be smooth — be fast.

Beginning of the catch - front view

The Power Phase

A good way to think of the power phase is to visualize that you are pulling the boat up to a paddle that is anchored vertically in the water, or to pretend that there are posts sticking up out of the water and that you are reaching forward and pulling the boat up to the post. Regardless of how you picture the process, you want to have your lower hand nearly in the water and your top hand loosely on the paddle top grip. Use your arms as levers to transmit the power from the torso to the paddle. The first portion of the stroke should come from the back and shoulder. Then, once the shoulder comes back to neutral, you follow through with the arms.

Keep your stroke short and crisp. Once the elbow of the lower arm reaches your hip, the power phase is over. Going beyond this point causes the paddle to lift upwards, pulling the canoe down — not forward.

Power phase

Photograph by Carl Caylor

In the power phase, Calvin Hassel (left) and Bob Rapant,
demonstrate why they are both national champions.

So, now you have the picture that in order to make the canoe go
forward, you've got to pull the canoe forward to an anchored
paddle. But there's more to it than that. You've got to also use the
drive down of the upper hand to keep the blade fully submerged as
the boat moves ahead. (This is called *loading* in canoe sprint technique.) Keep the top elbow high so that you can use the shoulder to
drive the paddle downward as the stroke develops. This will get the
most out of the power stroke.

**Keep the paddle vertical during the power phase.
The stroke should be in line with the keel line of the
canoe. Too often, paddlers tend to follow the side of
the canoe with their paddle. Bow persons' paddles
should enter the water a foot or so away from the
boat and come in so that the paddle nearly touches
the boat at recovery. Stern paddlers do just the
opposite, planting the paddle right beside the boat
and coming back straight.**

What are your legs doing during all this? It's obvious that they play a lesser role, but there are different schools of thought on how to use them. The most important function of the legs and buttocks is to lock you in the canoe. This way, you can transfer the power from your paddling directly to the boat — there's no slippage. (Canoe seats are padded not just for comfort. They are padded so that your butt doesn't slip around.)

Some paddlers lock their legs and only move them to loosen the muscles up before a portage. Others will "cycle" their legs as they stroke. Still others will fold a leg under the seat, shifting periodically. We recommend that beginners lock their legs in the canoe, using proper foot-braces and straps as we've outlined in Chapter 3.

Courtesy Le Nouvelliste

Some of the world's best paddlers demonstrate the forward stroke phases. Serge Corbin and Normand Mainguy (first boat) are in the power phase. Bruce Barton and Solomon Carriere (second) begin the catch. Patrick Lynch and Bob MacDowell (3rd) are at the end of the power stroke.

Recovery (front view)

The Recovery Phase

Just as there are several methods to get the paddle into the water, there are several ways to get it out. Some paddlers like to lift it straight up and out, others like to slice it out. We recommend that you slice it out by dropping your top hand, pushing the paddle forward, and lifting the lower hand up and out to the side. This will slice the blade out with minimal resistance and set you up in good position to rotate back to the catch position. An efficient recovery will also encourage you to keep the stroke short and crisp.

> **Don't keep your recovery the same speed as the power phase of the stroke. Watch the good paddlers — their recoveries are fast. The time your paddle spends swinging through the air isn't helping you at all. To go fast, you have to get that paddle back in the water where it will do some good. If you want to increase your stroke rate, do it by making quicker recoveries.**

Remember, the recovery phase is the "down time" of the stroke — it's the time when you are not driving the canoe forward. So don't fall into the habit of a slow recovery. Keep it quick.

To summarize the forward stroke: **Anchor the paddle in the water vertically and pull the boat up to that anchor. Do that by rotating the torso and folding the lower shoulder forward, reaching to slide the paddle into the water, and then use the torso to pull the boat to the paddle.**

Bow Paddling Technique

We recommend that newcomers start in the bow. Generally speaking, it is easier to learn the bow position because the majority of time, the bow paddler is concentrating on doing the forward stroke. Only in limited situations — a submerged log ahead, a sharp turn, or a near collision — does the bow person have to help turn. For the stern paddler, there's ususally more to do — you can't apply all your power to simply going forward. The stern paddler has to be constantly alert to the position of the boat and have a wide repertoire of subtle stroke variations to use to adjust the course of the canoe.

When in the bow, get the paddle in the water out in front of the bow wave — in the clean undisturbed water. You will, because the boat is narrower where you sit, be in a position to apply maximum power to the stroke. That's why most experienced teams put the stronger person in the bow. (It's no coincidence that most of the C-1 champions are bow paddlers — they are usually bigger and stronger and a C-1 favors that type of paddler.)

The bow person sets the stroke rate and should also be prepared to assist when necessary to turn the canoe sharply, make last minute course corrections, and cooperate in leaning the canoe.

Stern Paddling Technique

The stern paddler generally sets the overall course in the river. To do that requires not only the proper calling of switches but also constant subtle adjustments to the stroke. The stern paddler must focus on getting the paddle in the water as far forward as possible, in as close to the boat as possible. Since the canoe is wide in the middle, this often means that the paddle blade will hit the side of the canoe during the catch. A canoe with scratches on its side where the stern paddler has hit is the mark of a stern paddler who is keeping the stroke close to the boat.

The canoe tends to "go away" from the stern paddler. If the stern person is paddling on the right, the bow will tend to swing left, due to the leverage factor. If you and your partner are out alone in the river, you switch sides (or "hut") about every 6 to 10 strokes to correct this and maintain a straight course.

Courtesy of Cindy Lynch

Deep water allows you to use a slower, more powerful, stroke rate.

But there are many times, especially when you are riding someone's wake or in a pack of canoes, where the stern paddler has to dig into the stroke repertoire to keep the boat straight. Here, you're usually not as concerned about losing a bit of power, for you're riding with others, so you might use a subtle hook stroke or a modified J-stroke. This can be a regular forward stroke where, just at the end of the power phase, you put a little hook in. Or you may put just a tiny angle outward on the face of the paddle (a pitch blade stroke) as you pull it back. Either adjustment should bring the stern back in line without losing a lot of speed. A slight quarter draw is usually all that is needed to prevent the canoe from drifting the opposite way. These subtle strokes can help steer the boat in many situations when you are not worried about losing a little bit of energy and also help prevent having to switch sides all the time.

Paddling C-1 is a good way to learn the stern position. You are mid-way in the boat in a solo canoe and have to do everything yourself to keep the boat straight. You have to master not only a forward stroke but all the corrective strokes as well.

A few thoughts about switching sides. Because you are calling "huts" every 6-10 strokes, it's an action that has to be done smoothly and with little or no loss of time between strokes. All it takes is a little practice. Remember to call the "hut" at the beginning of the preceding stroke. Both paddlers then complete the power phase of that stroke before switching.

Stroke Rate

There is no "right" stroke rate. All other things being equal, a quicker stroke rate is going to result in a higher hull speed. But, especially for beginners, there is a limit — you can paddle only so fast before your technique comes apart.

Most teams paddle at a rate between 60 and 70 strokes per minute. Shallow water requires a quicker rate, while deep water allows you to use a slower, more powerful pace. The lower end for racing is around 50 to 55 while the maximum rate for most racers is about 80-85 strokes per minute.

Body size and strength come into play. Smaller men and women tend to use a quicker stroke rate than a big powerful paddler. You will find your optimum stroke rate as you gain experience.

When you start out in canoe racing, your technique will deteriorate quickly as as soon as you pick up the pace. As you get better, your optimum stroke rate will increase. You will find that you are picking up your recovery time faster and faster. Your power phase will stay about the same, but your recovery will be quicker. Settle into a stroke rate that is comfortable and efficient for you. As you polish your technique, your rate will pick up.

When you are novice and paddling with someone for the first time, try starting with the boat trimmed bow light or at least dead level in the water. It is much easier for the stern paddler to control the canoe when the bow is light. Too often, beginning partners have a heavy strong male in the bow and a small man or a light woman in the stern — and the boat is uncontrollable. Once the boat starts to swing, no one can bring it back. Just trim it up before you go and things will be easier.

Crew Coordination

If you watch enough canoe races, you'll be sure to see and hear some quarrelling crews come down the river snarling at one or the other over something that happened earlier. Compatible partners try to match up not only in such things as technique and stroke rate, but also in temperament and expectations. Be sure to paddle with someone who's fun to be with — often there's an inverse relationship between snarling and boat speed.

Setting The Pace

Finding an optimum stroke rate in a C-1 is fairly easy — you just have yourself to worry about. In a C-2, you have to find a stroke rate that fits both of you. This may take some time. Some people just don't match up well together; others seem to compliment each other's strengths.

In a C-2, there's no "captain." You are both making the boat move, and you are both steering the canoe. Each paddler has responsibilities: the bow paddler sets the pace and the stern paddler must stay with the bow paddler — even if you don't like what your partner is doing. That's when you communicate orally such as "pick it up" or "let's back off for a bit." You've got to stay together, otherwise you will have diminishing returns and will be just wasting each other's energy. If you are not in synch, your boat speed will drop dramatically. Make sure that you communicate—orally or by signals — when a change of pace is called for.

Making Switches

Listen to a pack of canoes coming down the race course and you'll hear "hut" grunted, spoken, or yelled. Most canoe racers use the word "hut" to call switches although you can use anything that is understandable. The stern paddler usually calls the switches.

You should call the hut before the boat starts to turn — anticipating rather than reacting to changes in heading. Call the switches at the beginning of a stroke and then switch at the end of the power phase. Once in a while, the bow paddler will be in "la la land" and miss your call. Priscilla Reinertsen says, "If my bow partner doesn't switch, I will have, but I'm always alert to compensate with weight balance or stroke technique." If you get caught suddenly paddling on the same side of the boat, it's up to the stern paddler to correct the situation, either by calling the "hut" again or by going back to the opposite side.

> **Sometimes, my partner calls a quick hut and I think, "wonder why he did that?" Then a big rock slides by the stern and I know. So trust your partner. It's the job of the bow paddler to see and avoid obstacles. The bow paddler should warn the stern paddler of things up ahead, by saying, for example, "rock on the right" or "log ahead" just as a lead cyclist might warn those behind of potholes or rough road sections. The bow paddler is always free to call switches whenever necessary.**

While the stern person generally calls the huts, the bow person should have the ability to call the huts at any time, particularly in shallow water or in stretches where there are a lot of logs and rocks. When you are wake riding, the bow paddler can often see the wave better or see the boat going off and should call the hut. While most teams switch every 6 to 10 strokes, you have to adjust to conditions — both paddlers should be able to call a hut at any time. C-2 means just that; work together.

Turning the Canoe

Ok, you can keep that sleek racing canoe going straight. But what happens when you want to intentionally turn? This is accomplished by leaning the canoe in combination with subtle adjusting strokes such as the quarter draw and sweep. Any time you utilize an adjusting stroke, you are losing some forward motive power. So whenever possible — particularly for gradual turns — a lean combined with normal forward strokes is all that you will require.

When leaned down slightly on its side, a marathon canoe will carve a turn just as a ski will carve when it is edged. The roll should be a steady and gradual one with the legs of both paddlers well braced against the inside of the canoe to prevent an unwanted swim.

If you lean the canoe down to the right, it will curve to the left and vice-versa. Turns made by leaning are gradual, although the more you lean, the quicker the boat will turn. The stern paddler uses the hips to initiate the lean and the legs to hold onto the boat. At the same time, one foot should lift up on the inside foot brace loop. (If you want to turn right, lean left and lift up on the right foot strap.) If you are in the bow, your natural inclination will be to counter any lean that your stern partner starts. Don't let this happen. Keep your hips loose and go with the lean.

C-2 partners are a team and must work together. The stern person usually leans the boat to the side being paddled on and thus is leaning into a paddle. On the other hand, the bow paddler is feeling very awkward, paddling on the opposite side of the lean. What you've got to do in the bow is relax the hips and not fight the lean — just keep the body loose and upright. Here's where trust comes in — if you are paddling in the bow you've got to know that your stern partner is not going to let the boat go over. These are the things you work on in practice to build that trust and confidence.

Don't lean the canoe with your whole body — just roll your hips and pull up with the leg. It is not unlike cornering on a bike where you lean the bike but keep your upper body vertical. It is also like cornering a ski, where your hips are out helping to carve the turn but your upper body is vertical.

So, use a lean when you want to maintain your forward speed and just need to turn gradually. But what about that rock or sharp bend up ahead? When you need to turn sharply, you've got to use corrective strokes that might kill a little momentum but which will turn that Kevlar beauty before disaster strikes. It's better to sacrifice a little of your forward speed than the canoe.

Another good way to turn while maintaining speed is to go to "sides" — having both racers paddling on the same side of the canoe. Turns are made by paddling on the opposite side from the direction being turned with a judicious use of a little lean. To go sharply left, both racers will paddle on the right and lean the canoe down on its right side.

Photograph by Dick Mansfield

A team working together to turn a C-2. Bow paddler quarter draws as stern employs a slight sweep. Both lean the boat right to turn left.

Quarter Draw

For the bow paddler in marathon racing, the most important stroke, after the forward stroke, is the quarter draw. (A complete draw is where you pull the paddle blade in perpendicular to your canoe.) For a quarter-draw, the paddle is placed partially in front and drawn in at a 45 degree angle toward the boat. The quarter draw is more efficent because it has a forward vector and helps move the boat ahead as it turns the boat. Stern paddlers also utilize the stroke in a variety of situations.

Let's say that a quick change of direction is needed. The bow paddler changes the stroke slightly, reaching forward and out, at about a 45 degree angle, drawing the bow up toward the paddle. If the stern paddler does the same from the other side, the turn is even more effective. To the observer from shore, these little "tweaks" are imperceptible. The canoe loses little speed and the paddlers are back to a forward stroke at once.

Full Draw

If you do some downriver racing and get into rapid water, you'll use the full draw quite often. A full draw kills your forward momentum since you are reaching out to the side, perpendicular to the canoe, pulling the boat out to the anchored paddle. It's more

Photograph by Carl Caylor

Two women C-1 racers turning left, leaning their boats
with hips and legs, keeping their bodies vertical.

radical and therefore, used only when really needed. A bow draw
is often accompanied by a stern draw or even a quick rudder if a
"bus stopping" collision appears imminent.

Sweeps
A sweep is aptly named. You do a forward stroke but do it in
a more circular method. You accomplish the sweep by starting your
stroke as normal, then using a sweeping, almost semi-circular
power phase, bring the paddle back to the normal exit point.

Sweeps are particularly effective in the stern of a C-2 and are,
along with leaning, a primary tool for the C-1 paddler.

Other Strokes
Once in a while, you may need to use a *pry*. This stroke is
opposite of the draw — you are pushing away from the canoe. A
bow paddler will need to pry in whitewater, but in a marathon race

boat, the stroke is rarely used, except in some waking situations. Rather than pushing away, it is often more effective to make a quick switch and then draw on the other side. At racing speed, you're more stable using a quarter draw or draw.

In the most extreme types of turns, such as a buoy turn where you absolutely have to turn in the shortest radius possible, you will want to use a *post* (also called a *high brace* or a *bow rudder*.) The post is described in the following buoy turn section.

Buoy Turns

In marathon canoe racing, one of the most commonly encountered challenges is the buoy turn. Nearly all canoe triathlons require the contestants to make at least one buoy turn. More and more canoe race organizers are including out and back routes and short loops in their races. This racetrack format gives spectators a good look at the race and, for paddlers who know how to do a sharp buoy turn, also presents a good opportunity to move up in the race standings.

The problem seems straightforward enough: execute a quick and sharp change in the canoe's direction, often 90 to 180 degrees. The problem is that marathon canoes are designed to go straight and to go fast. They are not designed to turn. The keel line of a marathon boat has no "rocker" and stubbornly resists any sharp turning maneuvers.

As a result, many racing paddlers do not do well on buoy turns. Few have mastered the art of sharply turning a marathon canoe and the result is wide turns and a huge loss in speed. This can mean the difference in a closely contested race. By learning to take buoy turns well, you will have a distinct advantage over most of your competition. It will enable you to catch and pass racers who may otherwise be faster than you at straight-ahead paddling. All it takes is the mastery of a few key techniques.

The Approach

When coming in toward a buoy turn — or any sharp turn — set your canoe up to approach approximately ten yards off to the side of the buoy, and initiate the turn five to ten yards before the buoy

Photograph by Kate Carter/Vermont Sports Today

Mark McAndrew and John Dostal set up for a buoy turn to the right.

is reached. Carry as much speed as possible into the turn and time your turn so that the bow of the canoe comes within a foot or two of the buoy.

The Brace and Roll

When the bow of the C-2 canoe comes within a few feet of the buoy, you should execute a "brace and roll" maneuver. First, the stern paddler should call the "huts" (or switches) so that the bow paddler is paddling on the inside, (closest to the buoy), and the stern paddler is on the outside. This will give you maximum turning leverage. Next, the bow paddler executes a high brace or "post" as it's called in marathon circles. (Some racers also find the cross draw or cross bow rudder to be effective.) This is a static position where the bow paddler holds the blade firmly in the water with the powerface of the paddle angled open, the leading edge pointed in the direction you want to turn, resisting the forward motion of the canoe. The more you angle the blade, the sharper you will turn. Your top arm should be high and out over the blade. The drag created by this high brace or post provides the pivot point around which the canoe will turn. At the the same time, the stern paddler uses some sweep or draw strokes to help the canoe pivot around the "post" set by the bow paddler. While all this is happening, the final and most important ingredient to the sharp portion of the buoy turn is to roll the canoe so that the outside gunnel (the side of the canoe farthest from the buoy) is leaned down.

Going To Sides

Once the canoe is approximately one-half to three-quarters of the way through the turn, the bow paddler should now "hut" (switch) to the outside of the canoe so that both paddlers are paddling on the same side — the side that is being leaned down. This will bring the canoe out of the turn quickly and will maximize acceleration. Be careful with both paddlers on the same side — this is no time to flip. Usually only a half dozen strokes are needed before you can switch and get back to the forward stroke.

Acceleration Phase

Once the canoe is nearly back on the correct line, the bow paddler should switch again so that now both paddlers are again on opposite sides of the canoe. Pick up your stroke rate in this last phase and hit the power so that the canoe accelerates out of the turn.

C-1 Buoy Turn

The same basic principles apply to a one-person canoe although now buoy turns are more difficult because there is only one paddler and that person is in the center of the boat. The approach is the same and you must lean the boat down to the outside while getting as far forward as you can. Of course, there's no bow paddler to set a post so you need to use a powerful sweep stroke on the outside of the canoe while keeping the boat steadily rolled down. Once around the buoy, level the C-1 off and accelerate with a quick stroke rate.

To execute a tighter turn around a buoy, sweep stroke until you are half way around and then, without changing your grip, cross the paddle over to the other side, setting the blade in the water as does the bow C-2 paddler during a cross draw or cross bow rudder. This is a cross draw for the C-1. It slows the boat down but it also may let you to cut inside other canoes and accelerate out to advantage.

Like any phase of canoe racing, buoy turn technique has to be learned through practice and repetition. So, throw a milk jug in your local river or pond and get out there and work on your turns. Retrieve the container as you make your last turn.

Getting Some Help

When learning any skill sport, whether it's driving a golf ball, skating on cross country skis, or getting a racing canoe to move fast, it pays to get some coaching. Until you get someone to say "That's it" for a particular technique, you're never quite confident about how you are doing. No written explanation alone can provide all you need to know about technique. An experienced set of eyes can help you lock in the correct canoe strokes early on.

Where do you go for help? Go to some races and talk to racers — many have a fine eye for technique. Go to clinics put on by canoe clubs and canoe racing groups. Don't be hesitant to ask for advice.

Get videoed. Everyone has access to a camcorder or video recorder these days so get some shots head on, from the side, and the rear. Study them, slow them down, and have a good paddler take a look as well. Watch some videos, such as Mike and Tanna Fries's excellent one on paddling technique and training.

Technique is the key to getting fast in a canoe. As we said at the start of this chapter, the things that happen when a paddle enters, moves through, and exits the water separate the front runners from the stragglers. So get the basics down right from the start. Once you have read about technique, watched some videos, and done some practice, get a "pro" to look you over. When that light bulb goes off and you realize that yes, this is it, this is how to paddle correctly, you will not only have more fun in a racing canoe, you'll want to add rear view mirrors on your boat to find your competition.

Chapter 5

Training
A Plan For All Seasons

"Motivation is what gets you started. Habit is what keeps you going."
                                                    Jim Ryun
"All preparation is performance, or performance to be"
                                                    Ralph Waldo Emerson

Training is a year-round proposition for successful canoe racers. National class athletes may train as much as 600 to 1000 total hours a year (300 to 600 hours "on water") while recreational racers typically accumulate 100-200 total hours a year (three to five hours a week.) But, whether you hope to be an elite paddler like Serge Corbin or Bruce Barton, or more realistically, a "weekend warrior" striving to do well in your age group, you should have a systematic approach to the process of conditioning for canoe racing. Some canoeists have specific plans and keep meticulous training logs. Others are pretty laid-back and do whatever workout they feel like doing that day. There are many ways to fit training into a busy schedule. So, before you quit your job and start a full-time workout regime, let's look at some ways to weave a realistic training program into an already busy life.

Planning To Train
What are the components of a training plan? First of all, it should be a mix of activities. "Cross-training" has become a buzz word for the 1990s and for good reason. In the past, many canoe

racers just piled up hours and hours on the water and then hibernated all winter. But these days, many canoeists, like runners, cyclists, and others, have learned that weaving such activities as weight training, skiing, running, mountain biking, and climbing into their training not only makes training more fun, it also makes one more fit overall and therefore less prone to injuries. Successful racers aim for a combination of strength and aerobic workouts to use before the racing season. Then, once the weather warms up, time is spent predominantly on-water with some off-water training.

A second component of a good training program is quality. There is only a limited amount of time available for workouts — you just don't have the time to pile up a lot of "junk" paddling. A shorter, quality workout beats a longer "lily-dipping" cruise. Work, family, and community commitments can really cramp your ability to train extensively. And the weather doesn't help in most parts of the country. During the winter, inclement weather and early darkness make it tough to find time to squeeze workouts into the work week. "Canned" training formulas just don't fit most people. So bend and adjust a training plan so that it fits you — your athletic abilities, your available time, and your goals in canoe racing.

> **Sometimes I only have an hour, twice a week, to paddle. After a warmup, I'll head into a 30-35 minute session of significant intensity, then a cool down. It's not ideal, but I can maintain my speed and hold on to my endurance for a shorter race. When time is short, emphasize quality.**

A third component of a good training plan is just that — a plan. You need to begin by analyzing where you are starting from and where you want to go. Once you have identified your strengths, weaknesses, and goals, you then need to establish a plan — a systematic approach — toward obtaining those goals. As Rob Sleamaker points out in his superb book *Serious Training For Serious Athletes*, "Systematic planning enables you to clearly identify strengths and weaknesses and develop strategies for improving these areas."

Designing Your Plan

Does having a systematic plan mean that you need a coach and an elaborate rigid training plan? Of course not. Some racers successfully use a laid-back approach to training, going primarily by the way their bodies "feel," and end up happy with their conditioning and their race results. Yet, if you look closely at the routines of the more successful racers, you will find that they have, over the years, developed some basic approaches to their training. Even if their training appears somewhat unstructured, it will usually include these basics:

1. A peak at a given time of year or for a particular race.
2. A hard/easy approach, alternating hard days with easier ones.
3. A good dose of intense speed work — intervals and Fartlek.
4. Once a week or so, a long, relatively slow over-distance workout of three hours or more.
5. "Listening" to their bodies and adjusting training accordingly.
6. Time for adequate rest and recovery.
7. A mix of activities over the year.

Photograph by Chris Wingender

Find a training plan that fits you -- your athletic abilities, your available time, and your canoe racing goals.

A "paddle as you go" training plan can easily be more structured if that is your inclination. Advocates of specific training plans and records — and there are many — want more discipline and organization in their training to make sure that they get the hours and the activities that they feel they need. They usually have a plan that includes "periodization" or varying training volumes by week and even months. Thus, a typical schedule aimed at a mid-August peak might build the activity, with some easier recovery weeks, during April, May, and June and then back off right before a key race. Athletes who cross-country ski might have a similar peaking period in February or March. This is the approach advocated by Rob Sleamaker.

The point is that whether you use a highly structured program or a more loosely defined plan, your training will benefit by having some direction. Each racer must decide how much discipline and organization can be tolerated and train accordingly. Let's look at some of the components that should be part of any training plan.

A key concept that should be considered in planning your training is specificity — exercises or activities aimed at training the specific muscles in your sport. In short, specificity means that the best training for paddling is to paddle. This may mean using a paddling or rowing machine in the off-season. It also can include specific resistance devices such as surgical tubing or weight machines used in such a way so as to build your canoeing muscles. And most of all, it means paddling — on the water. The object is to "lock on" your mind, your muscles, and your nervous system to a desired motion so that it becomes natural and so you can repeat it with strength, again and again.

Many who exercise find that a coach or personal trainer is helpful, not only to get them set up with good strength plans, but to push and encourage them in their training. Roberta Shapiro, a top masters paddler, cites the benefits of her one-on-one training, "I've learned a lot about myself, how far I can push myself. I don't get hurt as much — it keeps me from overtraining, both before race season and during it."

Knowing Yourself

In designing even the most rudimentary personal training program, it is a good idea to start by thinking about your own capabilities and interests. Are you a morning or afternoon person? Can you leave work early for a long mid-week paddle? How easy is it to find a partner to paddle with and an easily accessible place to canoe? How's your strength and flexibility? How many hours a week can you realistically spend training?

Training for canoe racing is more than just paddling until you're strong and fit. In order to go fast in a boat and be able to maintain good speed for hours at a time, you need to build endurance and strength, work on speed, and hone technique. So as we look further at training, we will break it down into these five important areas:

1. Aerobic Endurance Training
2. Anaerobic Threshold Training
3. Anaerobic Speed Training
4. Skill Training
5. Strength Training

Aerobic Conditioning

As in any long-distance event, in order to do well in canoe racing you need not only to be fast but to be able to use that speed effectively over a long period of time. Aerobic training can be thought of as the building up of an aerobic reservoir which is then drawn upon as canoeists race throughout the season. It is the training program that many coaches prescribe for running, cycling, or cross country skiing. First you build the aerobic base and only then, when you are well into your program, do you add the sprints and harder workouts to emphasize speed.

Aerobic training goes by many names: base training, endurance training, distance, or over-distance training. And whether your exercise session is 30 minutes or three hours, exercise physiologists and coaches recommend that you do most of your training in the *aerobic zone*. This zone, different for each person, is based on an estimate of your maximal heart rate (MHR).

Photograph by Dick Mansfield

Keep your heart rate in the aerobic zone during endurance training.

What's Your Aerobic Zone?

There are several ways to determine your maximal heart rate. One way to find out is to participate in a supervised treadmill test. Another is to go to a track and after a warm-up, run an all out mile and then take your pulse.

A simple method for estimating maximal heart rate (MHR) is to subtract your age from 220. Thus, for a 50 year-old, the MHR would be: 220-50 = 170 (MHR) The so-called aerobic zone, in which you want to do most of your aerobic training, is between 60% and 80% of the maximal heart rate, or in this example, 102 to 136.

A more accurate estimation method uses the resting heart rate (RHR). After you wake in the morning, wait a minute or so and then take your pulse. Do this several mornings and the average will be your resting heart rate. Let's assume that your RHR turns out to be 58. To find your aerobic zone, first subtract half your age from 205. Then subtract the RHR from that number, multiply it times .6 and .8, and then add the RHR back in. Estimating for a 50 year-old:

$$205 \text{ minus } 25 = 180$$
$$180\text{-}58 = 122$$
$$122(.6) + 58 = 131 \qquad\qquad 122(.8) + 58 = 156$$

Exercising below this range range has, in the eyes of many experts, little training value. Exceeding it during training for great lengths of time, which is easy to do if you are prone to overtrain, will probably detract from the aerobic base.

> **The heart rate charts that you see in health clubs and exercise books are based on estimates related to sex and age. I find that I am "off the chart" when I cycle, paddle, or ski. You probably will to. That's because trained athletes, regardless of age, usually don't fit into these standards. There is a new formula for "chronically fit" persons who have stayed active as they age and thus retain more of their cardiovascular fitness. If you fall in that category, your maximum heart rate, and the corresponding aerobic zones, will be a little higher. You should check with your physician or an exercise physiologist for a more specific estimate.**

Approximately 60% to 70% of your training time should be conducted in the aerobic zone. For long over-distance training sessions of two hours or more, keep the intensity to the lower end of this range, say 60% to 65% of your MHR. Try to get in an over-distance session once a week, if possible, especially in the early season. Endurance sessions of two hours or less should simply be below 80% of MHR.

It is tempting during aerobic sessions to push it a bit too hard, especially if you paddle the same course time after time. You don't want to make every workout a speed workout. You need to be aware of the kinesthetic cues that can keep you from over-doing it, that keep your workout aerobic. One way to do it is to learn what breathing patterns correspond to a particular heart rate. Another monitoring method is to take your pulse during and after a workout. This is not always easy to do, especially with a paddle in your hand. A better way is to use a heart rate monitor. More and more athletes, including those who choose not to race, but work out for fun and to keep their weight down, now use heart rate monitors.

In canoe training, a heart rate monitor can be used in several ways. The chief use is to keep your training in the appropriate range for the desired workout. For endurance training, this will be in the so-called "aerobic range" that was previously described. The system, which usually consists of a chest band and wrist readout, can be set for your specific heart rate range. It will beep when you are either above or below the range. This way, you can keep out of oxygen debt in fast time trials or conversely, make sure that you are not just "cruising down the river" and are keeping your heart rate up high enough to derive some training benefits. Another important use is to make sure, when you are paddling sprints in training, that you allow proper recovery time before the next interval. Heart rate monitors are now in an affordable price range — less than a good racing paddle. They make nice gifts for paddlers who are serious about their training.

Aerobic Endurance Training

Endurance training is something akin to an energy bank account. Over a period of time, through training, you slowly build up a balance which can, if you use it properly, be drawn down later in canoe races. When one exercises aerobically over fairly long periods of time, the body becomes trained to use more efficient ways to distribute blood, and oxygen. Capillaries, which may have been undeveloped, are brought into the action. This improved circulation is one reason that many heart risk patients are put on a regulated exercise program. For athletes, this process helps keep the exercise aerobic and helps muscles stay supplied with blood, promoting efficiency and also preventing cramping. You need about a two hour session of aerobic exercise to best promote the development of new blood vessels.

> **Long paddling sessions can get boring. If solo, bring a "Walkman" and paddle the first half of the session without music, focusing on technique. Then put on the music and get energized for the second half of the workout.**

Another reason for endurance training is to build up the body's capability to store glycogen and, at the same time, train the body to burn fat. Here's the way it works: you have basically two fuels for your endurance paddling muscles — glucose and fat. Glucose (glycogen) is the primary source of energy for race pace activity. The longer and harder you paddle, the more you burn. Exercise physiologist David Costill's studies on the muscle biopsies of swimmers have shown that these athletes had greater amounts of glycogen in their muscles than non-athletes. Experts such as Costill say that training changes the metabolism in the muscles, enabling the cells to store glycogen better. If you are well-trained, you can also replace the glycogen faster after a workout.

> **If you are serious about canoe training, you owe it to yourself to obtain a heart rate monitor. By knowing precisely how hard you are pushing yourself, you will train more efficiently and effectively.**

But, even if you go into an event well-rested and well-fueled with glycogen, there's only a limited amount that you can store — usually about two hours worth. After that, to use the colorful terms of competitors, you "bonk" or "hit the wall." Your engine has hit "empty" and it's time to slow down, re-fuel, or even quit the competition. So how do canoe racers go for eight hours or more and keep energized? First, they make sure that their training includes a good dose of long steady paddling to condition their body to burn fat as well as glycogen. Fats are not as easily used as glycogen, so you need to train your body to burn fats and thus stretch your glucose reserves — and the way to do it is with long distance training. Second, they learn to eat and drink at regular intervals during both long training sessions and races.

How long should endurance sessions last? For most racers, one to two hours per session will be sufficient, so long as you stay in the 60% to 80% of MHR range. Additionally, as mentioned before, we recommend one over-distance session of two hours or more every week if your schedule permits. Over-distance sessions will be critical if you plan on doing a long race of three hours or more.

Don't compete with others when training for endurance. It's really easy, when you are out with a bunch of canoes, to start picking up the pace, vying for the lead. That's fine when you are working on speed and tactical skills, but not when your aim is a steady endurance session.

Beginners and average paddlers often get more out of long training sessions than elite racers. It is a chance to work on strokes, wake riding, and reading the river, as you condition your paddling muscles.

Photograph by Dick Mansfield

Over-distance workouts are part of any successful racer's plan.

One trick used by some elite paddlers who want to train with friends who are less-accomplished paddlers is to add resistance to their canoe. Wrap a couple of rubber bungee cords around the bow and see how it works. By killing some of the glide of the canoe, it gives the better paddler a good aerobic workout but still allows the group to train together.

Like marathoners with their twenty-mile training runs and cyclists with their five hour Sunday rides, to be an accomplished canoe racer, you need to train for endurance and to include a long paddle in your weekly training plan. You need to get your body in the habit of efficiently adding and withdrawing energy and must get used to drawing from several accounts (the "fat" account as well as the "glucose" account), and you need to build up the bank accounts over a period of time so they are fully developed when race day comes. A program of long aerobic training periods, both off-water and on-water, is a key element in any successful canoe racer's training plan.

Anaerobic Threshold Training

As the intensity of your energy output increases, you will reach a point where your cardiovascular (aerobic) system and muscle enzymes cannot meet the metabolic demands of your muscles. Your muscle cells will not be able to process the lactate being produced and you begin to accumulate lactic acid. Welcome to what is called your "anaerobic threshold."

It is at this transition point that your body must shift over to its anaerobic system to obtain energy. Once you "cross the anaerobic threshold," the new energy system on which your body must depend will not last long — perhaps thirty seconds to two minutes tops. One of the keys, then, to any good training program, is an attempt to increase this threshold so that you can stay aerobic at higher output levels.

This can be done. We can all train our bodies so that our aerobic thresholds are pushed back, allowing us to work longer at higher intensity levels while still remaining aerobic.

We accomplish this by training at or slightly below the threshold level. In most athletes, that threshold is hit at about 80% to 85% MHR. Training at or just below this zone will improve the body's ability to buffer and recycle lactate as intensity levels increase. In short, you can push your anaerobic threshold higher — so that it won't be reached as easily during intense activity.

There are many ways to increase anaerobic threshold: running repeats on hills and running intervals on the track are two common methods. In the canoe, the best way is to do a series of long intervals or "surges." These are rather intense paddling segments or "pieces" that run between four to ten minutes in length, usually separated by a recovery period of one to two minutes. They are done at about 80% MHR.

> One thing that newcomers to canoe racing notice is that it's hard to push their anaerobic thresholds by paddling. Remember, you are just utilizing the muscles of the upper body, which don't have the same cardiovascular needs of the large leg muscles. Running, cycling, and cross country skiing will quickly spike a heart rate monitor. Yet, you will find that as your paddling technique and skill levels improve, you will be able to push your heart to the levels required for both threshold and full anaerobic training.

You can sprint (90% + of MHR) only for short periods of time, so increasing your anaerobic threshold — allowing you to effectively go faster for long periods of time — is crucial for any aspiring canoe racer. We recommend including one anaerobic training session per week in your schedule. Even if time is short, be sure to incorporate this type of workout into your plan.

Anaerobic Speed Training

Speed in a canoe is a combination of timing, technique, and power with a good dose of cardiac fitness thrown in. Usually, when discussing speed, canoe racers do it in terms of short term speed — the sprint to get into shallow water first, the dash for the finish line, the sprint to put the attack on a group of canoes riding your wake. As racers like to say, "In order to go fast, you have to train to go fast."

Speed conditioning has several objectives. First is to learn to become an efficient sprinter and know just how fast and how long you can go at a given speed. Second is to develop the strength and power to be able to move the boat fast.

Earlier, when we discussed the aerobic zone for training, we talked in terms of 60% to 80% of maximal heart rate. The anaerobic threshold, as we have said, generally occurs in the 80% to 85%

range. True speed training is done at 85% MHR up to complete maximum effort.

The Need For Speed

Racers, whether runners, cyclists, skiers, or canoeists, know that in order to race fast, you need to train your body to go fast. Speed is the thing that you should work on, especially if you have limited time in the boat. Speed in a canoe is a combination of technique, power, and conditioning. You don't make a canoe go fast by flailing at the water. If your technique deteriorates, you will not move the boat fast.

In canoe racing, speed is as important — if not more so — than endurance. To be successful, you must develop your speed to maximum potential. Here are some examples. Let's assume that you are racing and there are several canoes just ahead. If you can increase your speed, perhaps just for a minute or so, and catch them, you can then jump on their wakes and relax and work with them. Without speed, you are destined to stay back and slug it out on your own. Now you are coming to a portage. Without speed, you will be the last boat out every time. Likewise, without speed at the start of the race, you will never get an opportunity to ride in the lead packs — they'll be history before you know it.

> **When training time is very limited, speed training is especially important. Don't neglect it. One speed session of approximately 30 to 45 minutes per week will do wonders for your ability to get off the starting line and compete with some fast teams.**

Interval Work

Ugh! Only masochists like interval work, right? Well, if you like going fast in a racing canoe, you'll probably get to like, or at least appreciate, intervals. It's the way most elite paddlers get quick and stay quick.

When doing intervals, time, not distance, is your unit of measure. A mile upstream is much different from a mile downstream. So strap a watch to a thwart and do your intervals by time.

Speed intervals should be close to maximum effort (85% +) and can be shorter than a minute or as long as four minutes. (Save the longer intervals for anaerobic threshold work.) As we mentioned earlier, use a heart rate monitor if you can. This not only helps with maintaining the maximum effort but to helps gauge the recovery period between intervals, which are usually a minute or so.

Do a variety of speed intervals. For most racers, the shortest should be about thirty seconds to a minute. These "jumps" are done at near 100% MHR and train you to accelerate off the start line or to jump back on a wake. Longer speed intervals, one to four minutes, are done at the 85% to 95% range.

One of the best workouts (It feels so good when it's over!) is a ladder workout. Here you might start with a one minute interval, recover, then paddle a two minute interval, recover, and continue until you are sprinting for eight minutes. Then do the reverse sequence, with recovery periods. If you don't have a heart rate monitor to help, you'll probably need about two minutes recovery between the longer intervals and one minute between the shorter ones. The speeds in a ladder interval won't all be the same. The shorter sprints will be faster than the speed for the seven or eight minute intervals.

Speed intervals should be incorporated into some Fartlek workouts, picking random objects up ahead like trees or bridges, and sprinting for them.

Time Trials

Find a time trial course where the water is uniform depth and the current stays about the same. Here you can do standard runs, say once a week or every two weeks, to check for progress. Suppose you want to do a five minute time trial. Warm up and pick a prominent starting point. Paddle at sprint speed for five minutes and note where you finished — these are the two points you will use. Don't forget, in canoe racing time trials, we don't say to ourselves, "We've got to sprint for three minutes." We think, "We've to to get to the buoy first, let's do it!" So, get a fixed distance marked and then it is a matter of doing the sprint, recovering, and doing it again. Time trial courses are also good places to check out new boats, new paddles, or even new partners.

Photograph by Dick Mansfield

A program of interval speed work pays off on race day.

Speed Training On Land

Generally, anaerobic speed training is most effective when done paddling on water. But, if your boat time is limited, you should consider doing some anaerobic threshold training on land by running hills or doing some speed work. The anaerobic threshold of your cardiovascular system can be pushed upward with dryland training. Running and cycling are efficient ways to do this — by doing hill sprints, recovering, and doing them again, or by doing pure speed work.

You can combine sprints and portaging practice by stopping the sprint at the water's edge, running along the shore, and putting the boat back in. Make sure to allow time for a proper recovery before starting the next one.

The Armstrong Tests

In 1989, David Armstrong conducted the first (and only to date) systematic physiological testing of marathon racers paddling from a seated position. Armstrong, an exercise physiologist associated with the University of Maryland, is an active marathon racer.

The tests, conducted at the 1989 USCA Marathon National Championships in Marinette, Wisconsin, provided some conclusions that are particularly instructive when mapping out your training program. Utilizing a paddling ergometer which simulated marathon paddling, maximum oxygen consumption (VO_2 max), heart rate, and other factors were calculated for a number of racers. From these tests, Armstrong was able to determine that marathon canoeists are among the most fit aerobic endurance athletes involved in any sport. He further concluded that VO_2 max did not tend to decline until after paddlers reached the age of fifty.

From a training standpoint, Armstrong learned that most paddlers tended to train too often for too long at too low an intensity. Quality of training, not mere quantity, is the key — which is good news for paddlers living in the real world with only limited training time available. The test results also pointed to the fact that many racers do not incorporate enough recovery days into their program. "The majority of athletes we tested at the Nationals appear to be over-trained, or put another way, under-rested," noted Armstrong.

Generally, based on Dave Armstrong's studies, most racers should train harder for shorter periods and allow more recovery time.

Skill Training

Skill conditioning consists of working on good technique, hour after hour, so that you condition both your muscles and your mind to paddle well, not only during the first half hour of a race but in the last half hour. Good canoe racers practice their art, consciously thinking about how they are paddling and locking on to a good stroke. Then, on race day, when their minds are on the water, the competition, and race tactics, they won't have to think much about paddling. That skill will be conditioned in.

Skill training in the boat is a time to build trust and confidence. Why not, at the end of a training session, play in the boat for a few minutes, seeing just how far you and your partner can "lean" the boat before it goes over. Play in the waves and wakes of motor boats to get comfortable with handling adverse conditions. Explore the boundaries of balance in a safe setting. Also try slowing down your stroke rate, carefully examining each phase of your stroke.

Photograph by Dick Mansfield

"Play" in the boat at the end of training sessions to build confidence.

Be innovative. Ed Wagner is a new canoe racer. He and his partner Barry Moochler have a sheltered winding course where Ed, in the bow, paddles blindfolded, reacting to the commands of his partner in the stern. "It's great for getting a feel of the boat and the paddle," says Wagner, "and learning to trust your partner." Techniques like this might be a bit unusual, but if it helps improve your skill, go for it.

Strength Training

Canoe racing is an endurance sport which requires, in addition to a good aerobic "motor," a certain level of muscular strength. To be a successful canoe racer, you need to have both cardiovascular and strength workouts in your training plan.

Just as it is helpful to bring some organization to training in general, it also helps to be intentional about your plans for weight training. We think that you should, whether a fledgling paddler or an experienced one, have a year-round strength program. Not all athletes would agree with this, and many canoeists use weights only in the off-season. Yet most studies have shown that strength does not stay with you long once you stop the workouts. That's why it is smart to continue your strength program, albeit at a lesser "maintenance" level, during the season. All the plans we suggest will be based on a year-round program.

Efficient paddling calls for the use of the large muscles in the back and shoulders. These, the deltoids and trapezius muscles of the shoulders, the erector muscles of the back, and the fan-shaped latissimus dorsi muscles are the primary ones that you want to strengthen in a weight program. The triceps play a lesser role but also should be strengthened. Paddlers also need to work on the abdominals. As for biceps, pectorals, quadriceps, and calves — leave these to the guys and gals at muscle beach, or the folks who need them for their particular sport. If you have limited time for strength work, stick with the back, shoulder, and abdomen muscles.

Why do we need strength training? Many lithe women paddlers, as an example, move their boats with great quickness and certainly would not be thought of as weight room graduates. Yet, talk to a slim man or a petite woman canoe racer and you'll likely find that they work on strength. It gives them the power they need.

Strength training can include free weights, weight training machines, or simpler routines such as sit-ups and pull-ups. So, whether you use a bargain set of K-Mart weights in your basement or frequent a mirror-lined fitness spa, it's important to make your strength program fit your body and your objectives. If you're pressed for time, concentrate on the strength routines that are most specific for canoeing. The object of strength training is not to gain huge mass, but to increase strength and flexibility — to be able to have some power left at the end of a long race.

> **Power really counts in adverse situations. You'll run into many situations, from plowing up and over a wake to fighting a tough headwind, when the stronger canoeist has the advantage. Strength not only helps give the power needed for explosive starts or for cutting through a wake, it also allows you to keep paddling strongly, hour after hour. Most good paddlers learn that when they are fit, their muscles will fatigue before their cardiovascular system tires, and it is that knowledge that sends them religiously to the weight room.**

Getting Started With Strength Training

Whether or not you have used weights before, be careful about launching right into an aggressive strength program. If you are new to weight work, you should check with your doctor first. Likewise, unless you are experienced in lifting and strength routines, get some help from an instructor early on. You'll learn how to warm up before lifting, how to inhale and exhale during the movement, and how to use proper form. Having someone watch your form and get you started properly can prevent injuries later on. Once you are into a strength program, try to lift two to three times a week with a non-lifting day in between each session. As you begin, you may want to take 48 hours between sessions. As canoe season approaches, you should cut back to twice or even once a week.

> **Pull-ups are the key to many a canoe racer's success — just ask 1991 C-1 National Masters Champion, Ken Kolonich, whose strength training is almost exclusively pull-ups and push-ups. All it takes is a bar in a doorway and you are in business. Pull-ups and chin-ups strengthen the back and shoulder muscles. Vary the width of your grip on the bar and try some "bar-behind-the neck" pull-ups. Throw in some dips, situps, and push-ups and you have a strength routine that you can take anywhere.**

Free Weights

If you have the time to do a full body workout, fine. There are a number of excellent books on strength training which cover in detail the procedures for a comprehensive weight training regime. For canoe racers more pressed for time, we recommend a free weight program such as that which follows. Weights should be light enough to let you do eight to twelve repetitions of each exercise. Try to do three full sets. You do not have to do every exercise each session. Do six one day and the other six the next time.

Lat pull down — front or behind neck
Military Press
Upright row
Seated Cable Row
Back Hyperextension
Dips
Bent-over row (or bench row)
One arm cable press downs
One-arm dumbell row
Sit-ups
Pull-ups
Torso twists

Vary your workouts. One day add weight so that you reach muscular failure at about ten repetitions. Another day, go with lighter weights and higher (15-20) reps. One of the best ways to train with weights is a so-called "circuit" workout, where you move from station to station with relatively short rest intervals — usually forty-five seconds to one minute. This adds a significant cardiovascular component to your weight training.

> When time is tight, stick to the "Paddler's Big Five:"
> Lat pull downs — or pull-ups
> Seated Cable rows
> One arm cable press downs
> Dips
> Sit-ups

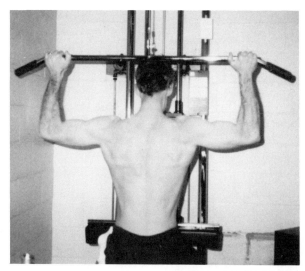

Photograph by Dick Mansfield

A lat-bar provides one of the best strength routines for paddlers.

Weight Machines

With the proliferation of exercise facilities in most of the country, it may be easier for you to find a weight machine setup then it is to either buy free weights or find a free weight gym. Universal or Nautilus-type operations are usually more "user-friendly" for the newcomer. Everything is purposefully controlled so it is easier to use the proper technique. Unlike free weights, there is no need for a partner or risk from falling weights.

Here is a sample workout using Nautilus. Weights should be set so that you can do eight to twelve repetitions using proper form.

Leg machine — used for warmup and for overall conditioning
Lat machine
Double Chest machine
Rotary Torso machine
Triceps machine
Pullover machine
Lower Back machine
Abdominal machine

Photograph by Dick Mansfield

When weight training, concentrate on the upper body.

Once well into the paddling season, back off to one or twice a week on the strength work. Come race season, it's time to stay with lighter weights, more reps, and fewer overall exercises. You should stop lifting altogether a week or so before an important race.

Whether you opt for weights or weight machines, plan to develop a strength program. Take the time to learn the exercises properly and start with low weights. Keep your objective in mind — you're not interested in pushing big weights; you're interested in pushing big wakes!

Early-season Training

For training purposes, it is best to divide up the year into sections or periods. You can do this any way it makes sense for you. We like to think of our training year beginning with early season paddling.

Once the ice goes out in northern climes, it is time to start thinking about hitting the water. If you have a decent aerobic base from the off-season and have been faithful with a strength program, you will be ready to start building endurance. Then, as you get comfortable in the boat, you can work on speed and acceleration skills. Ev Crozier, veteran canoe builder and racer, says he doesn't take a stroke in earnest until he has twenty hours in the boat.

Early spring workouts in the canoe should be easy-paced, aimed at building time on the water and working on technique, training muscles to get used to the paddling motions. If you are new to the sport, it is also a good time to get some expert advice and have some things to work on.

Fred Heese, author and expert paddler, calls spring "...the time to paddle ... for as many hours as your job, family, or other commitments permit. Start slowly ... so that your muscles get accustomed to paddling and so that you develop callouses, instead of blisters ... In this phase, your goal should be to build a good foundation of endurance."

If you plan to get on the water early, you'll want to make sure that you are properly dressed. Spring water temperatures are dangerous and there's always a chance that you could take an unexpected swim. Be sure to be wearing a polypro type top and bottom layered under wool. Also, carry some dry clothing in a water-tight bag. Stay close to the shoreline in the spring and try not to paddle alone.

Regardless of whether you plan to sit down with a coach or veteran paddler, and map out a detailed training plan for the coming months, or would rather just "do your thing" and skip all the regimentation, we recommend that you keep a training log. (There's a good chance, if you are active, that you already do.) There are many diary-type logs available or you can just use a notebook. Keep track of what you did, how long you did it, how you felt, and any other data such as weather, injuries, wildlife spotted, or race results. By keeping records, you can develop a sense of what training works for you or, if you get injured, what might have caused the problem. Not only do training logs provide valuable feedback for training, they also make good reading on a snowy evening when you recall that eighteen-mile race in hot, humid weather or the yacht that swamped you during a solo paddle!

Early season should be the time to work on your aerobic base and to gradually push back that anaerobic threshold. This calls for consistent doses of long, steady paddles at 60% to 80% MHR together with relatively long interval surges of five to ten minutes. At least once a week, you should consider doing interval surges of perhaps one of the following routines:

6 X 5 minutes	(one minute rest)
5 X 8 minutes	(1.5 minutes rest)
4 X 10 minutes	(2 minutes rest)

If at all possible, try to get in an over-distance workout of two to three hours or more once each week. Taper off the strength training to maintenance levels.

Race Season Training

As you enter the race season, you should gradually add more anaerobic threshold training and more pure speed work (anaerobic) to your program. If you are racing regularly, the races will provide much of the intensity you need. One day per week should emphasize short duration speed work. Try some intervals from the following sets:

30 X 1 min	(30 sec. rest)
20 X 2 min	(45 sec. rest)
10 X 3 min	(60 sec. rest)
1-2-3-4-5-4-3-2-1 ladder	(60 sec. rest)
20 X 30 sec (jumps)	(30 sec. rest)

These are suggested intervals that work for many paddlers. But experiment — find out what works for you. During racing season, be sure to allow one full day of rest per week and one very easy day (1.5 to 2 hours at steady 65%-70% MHR). Continue light maintenance strength training and try to fit in a run or cycle perhaps twice a week to stay ready for the portages.

If work and family obligations allow only two on-water training sessions a week outside of racing, take heart. You will do fine against all but the elite. Just be sure to devote at least one of your sessions to some intense intervals or Fartlek training. Maximize your on water time and do some aerobic cross-training when not in the boat.

Using Races For Training

Too many paddlers go to every race, big or small, and race all out. Others race only occasionally, preferring to train alone. A better plan is to use some of the smaller, local races as speed training and skill sessions. Have a game plan before the race — perhaps it will be to stick with the lead pack, or to just pick a group and stay with them, even if you can beat them. What you want to work on is speed and tactics.

Photograph by Dick Mansfield

Use local races to work on skills and tactics.

The first mile is critical in a canoe race. Often, you can take the placings after a mile and find that they have changed very little at the race's end. Use training races to work on your starting procedures. Get off the line with speed and work hard for the first mile or so. Then plan to work on tactics, waking, and sprints. Find a team that you can work with, even if means slowing down and waiting. Work with them under race conditions and then sprint at the end.

It's not that big a race so why not let the team behind, which you know you can beat (you're already ahead), catch up? Try to ride their wake. Try to drop them at a couple of corners, then join back up, and attack again at another spot. You've got to learn to do that to build confidence so that when a boat is right with you and going about your same speed, you will have experience in reacting appropriately. This is hard to do in training. Use some races that are not important to you for this practice and don't worry about where you finish.

> **Time after time I'll go to a race and see a boat that's twenty yards ahead of one team and thirty yards ahead of another. They can't catch the front team and just stay out alone the whole time. They end up with a wonderful time trial but they haven't improved their sprint speed or their tactics. Use some local races as an opportunity to work with other canoe teams and practice the tactical aspects of the sport.**

Peaking

While it's smart to ease off your training a few days before any serious race, when you are approaching the "big" race — the race you have been pointing for — your training intensity should be at a peak. Then you need to take time to recover or "taper" as you approach race day. Take up to a week beforehand to taper — quit strength training and long workouts. Keep sessions short, fast, and crisp. Increase your rest and recovery time. Come to the line as fresh and fit as possible.

> **After the rigors of a heavy season, I usually like to take a month or so almost completely off from training. It's a time to fully recover and to just get away from training for a brief period. Recharge the batteries and look forward to winter.**

Photograph by Inner Mountain

"Taper" your training as your approach a big race.

Off-Season Training

Off-season conditioning is one of the major differentiations that separate paddlers. If you paddle all summer and fall and then turn into a couch potato over the winter, you'll tend to lose conditioning at about the same rate you previously gained it. So, come spring, you will be starting out from scratch and well behind your racing friends who maintained their weight and their training once the water got too cold to paddle in.

Your off-season program is tied into your motivation, access to equipment and facilities, and in the north, your interest in wintertime outdoor activities. All in all, this is the off-season and for most, the training hours will be cut back and it will be a time to get away from paddling for a bit. It's a time to rest and to try other cardiovascular activities. It is also a time to work on strength and power through weight training.

Off-season Aerobic Training

Off-season training options for canoe racers are numerous. There are many activities that you can chose to stay in shape. Some paddlers chop and stack firewood, others snowshoe, others ice skate. Anything that gets your heart pumping and keeps it active for an extended period will help endurance. Throw in a little strength training and keep track of what you've done and you've got an off-season training program. Here are some popular choices of many canoe racers.

Off-season Running

Running in the off-season may involve slogging through the slush if you live in snow country. Yet, when the elements allow, running is, as every runner knows, an efficient use of time. You can get aerobic fast and get a good workout in without needing access to exercise facilities or special equipment. Canoeists can squeeze a 30 minute run into about any day, regardless of how many other things are going on in their lives.

Running is an excellent way to maintain a minimum aerobic base during the off-season. All it takes is a little motivation (sometimes the most difficult ingredient to find), a good pair of running shoes, and some cold weather gear. Run several times a week if you can and just cruise, keeping your pulse rate well into the aerobic zone. Get a reflective vest since you will likely be out after dark and run defensively.

If you are near an indoor track, see about running inside. Another indoor possibility is a treadmill. A newer and more popular option is the stair climbing machine. This will give you a good workout in 15-20 minutes and do so without the pounding of running. They also, because of their programming possibilities, seem to be less tedious than treadmills.

Running outside can be difficult and not much fun. Running inside is often boring. Many canoeists put away their running shoes in the winter and take up the sport that is most compatible with paddling — cross country skiing.

Cross Country Skiing

Many nationally-ranked canoe racers, both in Canada and the United States, are accomplished cross country ski racers in the off-season. Go to a major nordic race and you'll see many paddlers among the early finishers. For such athletes, the two sports go hand in hand — not only do the seasons fit together well but the sports are quite compatible in regards to muscle use and endurance.

Cross country skiing, like canoe racing, has changed a lot in the last decade. Not only has the technique of skating become dominant, the equipment is now light and fast, and for racing gear, expensive. The carbon fiber material used in paddles also makes up the ski poles of racers. Racing skis and clothes are splashed with wild colors.

Courtesy of Salomon

Many canoe racers also compete in cross country ski races.

If you live near snow, cross country skiing provides about the optimum endurance workout. Nordic skiing, since it involves both upper and lower body muscle groups, allows a thorough non-pounding training experience. If you wear a heart rate monitor, you will find that it is easy to arrive at and maintain your rate in the desired zone. And, if you choose to purchase roller skis or training skates, you can ski even when there is no snow. One does not need to race — you can go on long tours, have lunch along the trail, and still get a good workout in. This aspect of skiing is attractive to those who are ready to quit racing for a while.

The chief drawback for canoeists who are new to skiing is the skill required to enjoy the sport and get a decent workout. Cross country skiing does, like canoeing, take some time and practice to become comfortable. Here's what we recommend for newcomers:
1. Get someone knowledgeable to work with you — learn the proper technique.
2. Buy good equipment. It will be faster, lighter, and more fun.
3. Work with a sports shop that knows the sport.
4. Learn to skate on skis. The technique is very compatible with paddling and is the fastest way to travel on skis.
5. Try to ski or run several times a week in the off-season.

For paddlers with downhill skiing experience or who already cross country ski, we recommend that you try some ski races. They help keep you motivated. In most parts of the snow belt, there are many low-key citizen races around that can provide some spice to your winter training program. Come March, when ski racing season is wrapping up, you will be fit and ready to begin your early season paddling program.

Off-season Cycling

Cycling is a good non-pounding aerobic workout. But, like running, cycling off-season is controlled by where you live and your inclination to battle the weather. It is possible, especially with a mountain bike, to pedal nearly all year in many parts of the country.

Many paddlers ride indoors. It can be boring, but you get a good workout on a wind trainer or stationary bicycle. You can read a book, watch television, or listen to your choice of music on a headset. Bill Gardner, writing in the Connecticut Canoe Racing newsletter, describes his winter morning: "Every day before breakfast, I go for a 30 to 60 minute easy spin on my exercise bike with coffee, orange juice, two newspapers, and the CNN Business News. I sweat like a moose and shower and stretch afterwards."

Photograph by Dick Mansfield

Mountain bikes can be used for aerobic training year-round.

Rowing/Paddling Machines

Rowing machines are, like stair climbing machines, common equipment at fitness centers. They are also the home workout choice of many people. And, like stationery bikes and treadmills, they can be boring. It is hard, even for the most motivated athletes, to get more than 20 to 30 minutes on the machine. Yet, for canoeists, rowing machines like the Concept II are a great full body workout.

Paddling machines are designed to be even more specific to canoe racing. They are less common and somewhat difficult to obtain commercially. If you can find one, it is a good option for indoor off-season training — not necessarily for working on technique but for getting an aerobic workout while strengthening many specific canoeing muscles.

> **A Walkman cranked up with some good tunes or a TV is a must when on a rowing machine or paddling machine. Get fired up and go for some real intensity. John Mathieu likes to call this "good pain."**

When you make decisions as to what your goals in canoe racing are and how much time you can devote to training, keep in mind the five basic components we discussed: 1) Aerobic Endurance Training; 2) Anaerobic Threshold Training; 3) Anaerobic Speed Training; 4) Skill Training; and 5) Strength Training. These elements should be part of your plan, but most of all, do your own thing. Don't match the workouts of friends — unless you want to. Mix up your activities, keep things fun. Listen to your body, eat well, and get plenty of rest. Above all, don't necessarily try to force yourself into a training schedule that some elite racer published — make it your own. Training plans must be individual. Once you come up with a plan, don't be a slave to a schedule — keep the fun and spontaneity in training.

Concentrate on speed, learning the magic of "making that boat sing." Once you develop speed in the boat, you'll get enthused about canoe racing and find more time to paddle. And by mixing activities, varying workout intensities, and putting some play into your training, you'll enjoy getting in shape to race. When race day comes, you'll be in the right mental and physical condition to move that boat — fast.

Chapter 6

Reading The River
Life In The Fast Lane

"The canoeist must take the canoe where he or she wants it to go, not where it wants to go."

Bill Mason

All successful canoe racers know that rivers and lakes are filled with fast lanes and slow lanes. Whether cranking through the turns of Michigan's Ausable River, pounding through the waves of the Spokane River in Washington, or simply looking for the deepest possible channel in New York's Upper Susquehanna River, canoe racers all face the same fundamental problem — how to read the river. Taking advantage of a river's currents and eddies can often spell the difference between winning or being an "also-ran." This chapter will help you learn how to find the "passing lanes" and how to utilize the ever-changing conditions of wind and water.

We can never overlook the fact that the medium through which we race is a fluid one. Our "fluid race track" is constantly changing as it is affected by gravity's pull, the wind, and obstacles around, over, and through which it must flow. It is this ever-changing aspect of our rivers and lakes which is one of the factors that makes canoe racing so interesting. The fluid courses on which we race are constantly throwing new looks at a paddler, different problems and constantly changing sets of circumstances — all of which the racer must try to utilize to the best advantage. The racing team that knows how to find and utilize these currents and eddies will stay a step ahead of the team that mindlessly paddles down the course.

The Variables Encountered

There are five major variables that you should keep in mind when looking for the fastest course in any river or lake. These are:

1. current
2. water depth
3. width of the river or lake
4. obstacles in and along the race course
5. wind.

Of these, current and depth tend to be the variables which come into play most often and which have the greatest impact on your paddling strategy. We will analyze these variables and discuss how each has an effect on your course selection in three common racing situations: racing downstream on a river, paddling upstream on a river, or racing on a lake. Since most of your canoe racing will likely be downstream on a river, let's first take a closer look as to how the variables of current, depth, river width, obstacles, and wind can create fast as well as slow lanes while moving downstream.

Racing Downstream

To get an idea of the general rules, let us first look at a fictional river which is about 50 yards wide and straight as an arrow. Generally, the river will be deeper and the current will be faster in the center portion. This is where you would want to be if racing downstream. As you move to the sides of our fictional river, the river will gradually shallow and the current will slow.

One of the earliest lessons I was taught as a youngster concerning water was that streams and rivers flowed downhill. This seemed to make a lot of sense to me until a few years later when I was standing next to a fairly rapid moving little river and threw a large stick in the water, only to find the stick flowing back upstream near the bank. This was one of my first occasions to learn that nearly every rule has an exception. In this case, my stick was caught in an upstream eddy and it was being pushed back upstream by the eddy currents. So it is with almost all rules of the river. There are general rules and then there are the exceptions to the general rule. But that is what makes it interesting.

The technical reasons for all of this are complex and it's not necessary for us to get into it here but it is important to know that the current of any river is greatly affected by the river bottom. If you know what the river bottom is like, you will generally know what the currents are like. In simple terms, the friction between the shallow bottom and the water, causes the water to slow down. It also causes helical (corkscrew) currents along the shore. Where the bottom of the river is farthest away from the water's surface (where the river is deepest) the current will generally be fast. Where the river bottom approaches within several feet of the river's surface, the current will slow and be more directly affected by rocks and other items on the river bed.

Photograph by Dick Mansfield

"Cut the corner" on gradual turns in slow moving water.

Gradual Turns

Now let's throw a gradual turn into our fictional river. You will find that centrifugal forces carry the current to the outside of the turn. It is here, on the outside of the turn, where the river will generally be deep and the current fast. On the inside of the turn you will normally find a gradual shallowing bottom and slow current. Does it then follow that you should always stay to the outside of turns? The answer is: <u>sometimes</u>. In a gentle turn, the shallows on the inside will probably be simply slower moving water and if you feel fresh enough to sprint over the shallow water, you can often go faster by taking the shorter line of cutting the corner. This is where

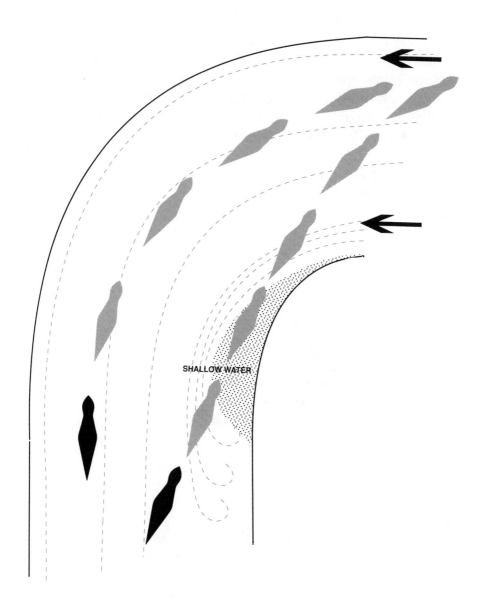

SHALLOW WATER

It is faster on some gradual turns to take an outside route, staying in the main current. In other cases, it pays to take the inside route and sprint through the shallow water.

the width of the river comes into play for if the river is large, it often makes no sense to swing far to the outside simply to pick up faster water. If the difference between the speed of the current on the outside of the turn and the speed of the current on the inside of the turn is great, then staying wide may be warranted. If it is not, stay inside and "cut the corner." However, if you are tired and no longer able to sprint, the outside route will be the way to go. Every turn, whether sharp or gradual, will require the racer to make a judgment call about the current differential — that is the difference between the speed of the outside current versus the slower speed (but shorter distance) of the inside current. As the overall speed of the river increases, so will this critical current differential. When in doubt, stay center or slightly inside of center. If the differential is extreme, it may be worth going the longer outside distance to catch the fast water. If not, stay inside and sprint!

If you are back in the pack, watch the canoes ahead. See how they handle the turns in the river — go to school on them.

Photograph by Tricia Heed

The bow paddler quarter draws as this team stays just outside the eddy line on a sharp turn.

Sharp Turns

Now let's take our fictional river and put a severe turn of 90° or more into it. Things really heat up now because the centrifugal forces carry the majority of the current to the outside causing a great deal of turbulence as the current hits the bank and rebounds into the river. Meanwhile, on the inside, the sharpness of the angle will normally create a substantial eddy behind the inside point of land. These eddies can be fairly violent in powerful current and you will often notice a distinct "eddy line" between the fast moving down-stream current and the upstream moving water within the eddy. It is important to be able to recognize this demarcation between the two currents. Often the best route is to ride just to the downstream side of the eddy line, taking advantage of the current without letting your canoe get into the eddy. The bow paddler must be careful not to let the bow cross into the eddy line, or the canoe can spin violently upstream, causing you to lose time, or even take the big swim.

On a broad river with gentle current, it may be to your advan-tage to actually pierce the eddy line, taking your canoe completely into the eddy, cutting the corner across the eddy and then angling back to the center of the river, picking up the downstream current again. To do this, both paddlers must be alert when they cross into the eddy. The move must be a powerful and intentional one. Both paddlers should be prepared to counteract the natural river forces that will want to spin the canoe until it is entirely within the eddy. This usually means a quick brace on the outside by the bow person, with a few sweep strokes by the stern person until the canoe has completely entered the eddy. Generally, however, the fast lane will be found just outside the eddy line while cutting the corner.

Finding Fast Water

If you haven't had a chance to scout the river ahead of time, there are certain things to look for to help you find the deeper, faster water. If the river is moving slowly, it will be difficult to pick up any telltale sign of shallows until you are actually in them. Sometimes you can notice a slight increase in the current speed over shallows — even in slow moving rivers. On the other hand, if the current is moving at a decent clip, you can often see "ripples" over the shallow water stretches. The deep water sections will usually appear dark and flat — unless the deep channels come among rocks or shallows. Here, look for telltale inverted Vs, with the open part of the V facing upstream and the closed pointed part of the V aiming downstream. Go for the V's and avoid the ripples.

Another signal for deeper, faster moving water is high banks. If you are proceeding down the river and one side has a higher bank than the other, it is usually due to deeper, faster, current action. In such a case, you would want to paddle to the side of the river that has the higher banks. Conversely, gradual, sloping, or sandy banks, are telltale signs of major shallow water areas.

Photograph by Tricia Heed

Look for the downstream V's in Class 1 chop and fast water.

Be aware that some rivers don't follow the usual rules. For instance, there are numerous rivers in upstate New York and certain parts of the Midwest that have riverbeds which tend to crown in the middle and drop away deeper to the outside. Thus, the current is often shallowest and slowest in the middle while being most rapid on the outside edge. This anomaly often occurs where the current is moving swiftly so you are usually able to pick out the shallow water in the center by the telltale ripples. The swift shoreline current should be clearly visible with the usual downstream V formation.

A good way to determine where the deeper, faster water is running is to "look for the bubbles." Often the faster current creates air bubbles, and you can follow those right down the fast lane.

Obstacles

To state the obvious, make sure that you avoid obstacles in the river such as rocks, logs or bridge abutments when paddling downstream. Encounters with such obstructions will often be of the disastrous kind. They can not only slow you down but also put you out of the race by damaging your hull.

The bow person is primarily responsible for being sure that the canoe misses obstacles since he or she is in a better position to see immediately impending obstructions. A quick draw is all that is usually required to stay clear of the problem. The stern person must react and keep the back of the boat where it ought to be — right behind the bow. If the current is slow, it is easier to miss obstacles, but sometimes more difficult to see them. Rocks or "dead head" logs will not be immediately evident if they are lurking just below the surface in still or slow moving water. For this reason, the bow person must always be alert to these hidden dangers. As current speed picks up, the obstructions will cause small waves, an eddy, or some other disturbance in the water right behind them which will tip you off to their location. Yet, because the current is more swift, the bow person has to be even more alert, as the time to react will be much shorter.

The most dangerous obstacle you will face is the "sweeper" or "strainer"—usually a fallen tree with its roots in the bank and its branches hanging in the river. The current passes through this obstacle—but your canoe will not. The current (even a slight one) can pin both canoe and paddler. The best medicine is avoidance. These sweepers are usually found on the far outside of turns where

Courtesy of Dick Foster

Obstacles can not only slow you down, they can end your race.

the current is undercutting the river banks. If you do not know what is around the next sharp bend, err to the center or inside. This is probably faster anyway.

> **In an emergency with an obstruction such as a "sweeper", both paddlers should backpaddle and attempt to slide or "set" the canoe to the inside of the turn. If all else fails and you tangle with a strainer, lean downstream — into the branches of the tree — to try to prevent the current from pulling the upstream side of the canoe down beneath the river surface. If the canoe goes under, attempt to climb up on the branches and await help. You can order another canoe!**

Wind On The River

The final major factor that can affect your course selection while paddling downriver is wind. The wider the river, the more that wind will come into play. The best way to avoid the effects of wind is to stay near the banks of the river, particularly if these banks are lined with trees. For example, if the prevailing wind is coming from the left side of the river, it will be to your advantage to paddle on the left side — sheltered as much as possible from the crosswind. But even if you are going into a headwind or being pushed by a tailwind, paddling near the river bank will lessen the wind's effects.

If the river is wide enough and the wind is severe enough, it can cause major problems. The best thing to do in a high wind is to hug the shoreline and slide your seats back. Moving the seats back in either a C-2 or a C-1 will have the effect of raising the bow and giving you a bit more steering leverage. If the river is so wide that the waves become incredibly heavy, you may even want to consider switching positions in a C-2, putting the lighter paddler in the front. In a C-1 you have to be prepared to push your seat back and begin paddling a great deal on one side. Don't be afraid to go back to a J-stroke in extreme situations.

Racing Upstream

Canoe races and triathlons are increasingly going to a loop format where the canoe course starts and finishes at the same location. This simplifies matters for organizers and allows specta-

Photograph by Dick Mansfield

Racers stay close to shore as they work their way upstream. Note the large waves thrown on the very shallow water near the river bank.

tors a better view of the course. What it means to canoe racers is that a significant portion of the canoe course will be upstream, <u>into</u> the current. And while the current is the canoeist's friend, something that should be sought out and utilized when paddling downstream, the current becomes the canoeist's deadly enemy when you are heading upstream.

Racing upstream not only requires the canoe racer to take most of the rules learned in paddling downstream and do just the opposite, it also presents its own unique set of challenges. For example, to paddle successfully upstream, you must pay much more attention to the precise line you are paddling. Likewise, you need to have an astute sense of current and water depth. It is the interaction of these two key factors, current and water depth, that you must continually monitor to find the fastest possible line upstream.

Wind is less often a problem or a factor in upstream work, as the canoe racers are almost always near shore, sheltered from the wind. Likewise, obstacles in the river play much less of a role in choosing your course as the overall speed of the canoes in upstream work is slower, and the current is not bringing you down quickly upon an obstacle. Large obstacles, such as bridge abutments or points jutting out from shore can be of significant help to the upstream paddler since these obstacles create eddies. These are the same eddies that usually are avoided when going downstream, but are just the ticket for assisting the canoe racer in staying out of the current on an upstream journey.

It is obvious that you must battle the current to go upstream. The idea is to minimize the current effect by staying relatively close to shore and by utilizing eddies whenever possible. How close to shore will depend upon the speed of the current coming downstream and the water depth near shore. Essentially, the canoe racer is looking for that fine line where he or she is staying out of the heaviest current but also in the deepest water practicable. The heavier and more swift the current, the closer the canoe racer will want to stay to shore, even if it means having to sprint through constant shallow water. If the downstream current is relatively slow, you will want to trade off facing minimal current so that you can avoid the real shallow water. It is a series of constant judgment decisions and you must vary your position throughout the course, depending on the current and water depth in the specific location.

Here are a few rules of thumb to follow when trying to find the fastest possible upstream route. First, if one riverbank has a number of undulations in it and the other riverbank is relatively straight, stay to the side with the undulations for there will be many eddies created by those undulations and points of land. Any time a river turns, you will almost always want to be on the far inside of the turn where there will likely be an eddy or backwater. This area will normally be shallow so you must be prepared to sprint.

When proceeding around sharp corners on an upstream course, it is important for the bow person to hold the bow in towards the shore because the downstream current will tend to push the bow out toward the middle of the river. C-1 paddlers will have to lean their boat and be alert to keep their bow headed directly upriver or slightly in towards the shore on the sharp bends.

If at all possible, keep your canoe moving directly upstream. The only time you want to be moving across the current is when you intentionally move from one side of the river to the other. This usually occurs when you are on one side and the river then turns the opposite direction, forcing you to change sides to take advantage of the upcoming slow currents on the inside.

When you make your move to cross the river, never paddle directly across, e.g., perpendicular to either bank. Rather, you want to cross the river at a gradual angle of about 20° or 30°. This will present enough of the upstream side of the canoe to the current to help push it across to the opposite side without causing you to lose significant forward momentum.

When should you cross? That can only be answered by the particular circumstances of the river on which you are paddling. If there is a substantial eddy below a sharp turn in the river, it is often beneficial to cross early so you can take advantage of that inside eddy on the opposite shore. If the turn you are coming to is relatively gradual, and the differential between the fast current and the slow current is not great, you may want to stick to the bank you were on until the last minute and cross "high" on the turn.

Upstream Tactics

Paddling upstream creates a unique set of technical challenges and solutions. Many racers find that trimming the canoe slightly more bow down than is usual for deep water will help the canoe track while going upstream and tends to be a bit faster. Passing another canoe while proceeding upstream is often difficult, particularly where the current is significant. Here you must choose between trying to get by the overtaken canoe to the "open" side (toward the center of the river) where the water may be slightly deeper but the current will be heavier, or to the "closed" side (next to shore), where the current will be less yet the depth will assuredly be less. When the current is barely perceptible or slow-moving, it is often better to opt to the open side. When the current is substantial, you have little choice but to try to pass on the closed side. From a strategy point of view, it is easiest to sit on the leading canoe's stern wave, waiting for it to zig slightly enough away from shore to give you an opening. When you make your move, do so with vigor. The wave you throw up by passing to the closed side will be hard for the other team to ride and it is likely that they will drop back.

Experienced canoe racers look at upstream paddling with relish. It's a time when the paddlers who possess more sophisticated paddling skills as well as the ability to find the best compromise between water depth and opposing current can really excel.

Lake Racing

When racing on lakes and other large bodies of water, current is naturally eliminated as a variable. There are few obstacles and any shallow water, if you find it at all, will be found close into shore. The big hurdle to negotiate in lakes and other large bodies of water is wind and the waves created by the wind.

Courtesy of Cindy Lynch

Heading into big water, these women paddlers move
their seats back and cover up as allowed in pro racing.

When racing a big lake, wind can come at you from all points
of the compass, and usually will. You will discover that it is easier
to keep the canoe straight when paddling into a headwind or a
frontal-quartering wind. In these circumstances, you do not have to
make many adjustments, unless the waves become so large that
moving the trim backward in the canoe is required. By sliding either
the bow person, the stern person, or both back, the bow will rise
more easily over the incoming waves, and you'll be less likely to fill
the canoe. If things really get heavy, it's sometimes advisable for
the bow person and stern person to switch positions, putting the
lighter person up front. In the worst possible conditions, move the
seats back, open your bailer, and do your best not to go directly into
the waves. By quartering into the waves at a 45° angle or more, the
boat will have a tendency to lift over the wave rather than plowing
through it, resulting in a lap-full of water.

A slight breeze coming from the stern is not a problem and will
actually push you along at a slightly higher clip. However, when a

stern wind begins to pick up and your canoe is being hit by following waves, the stern tends to lift with the result that the canoe suddenly pivots and goes left or right. This can be annoying, slow, and even dangerous. First, to fight the tendency of the canoe to pivot, again it would be beneficial for one or both the paddlers to move their seat position back. This will get both paddlers a little more leverage in the following seas. Second, the bow paddler will often have to hold a static high brace or active draw in order to help prevent the canoe from sliding radically left or right. The stern person will sweep on the opposite side, and this will assist in preventing the canoe from slipping to one side or the other. Another alternative is for the bow person to keep paddling while the stern person braces, rudders, and paddles — whatever is necessary to go straight and keep the bottom side down. If the canoe does get turned sideways to the wind, both paddlers will want to draw the canoe back around, heading away from the wind as soon as possible.

For the C-1 paddler, following seas are even a bigger problem. Here again, backing off on the seat will provide a little leverage and the C-1 paddler will end up paddling on one side or the other. You may also have to resort to a J-stroke or a rudder in order to keep the canoe from slipping badly left or right.

A heavy wind coming from the side is particularly frustrating to both C-2 and C-1 paddlers. In a C-2 boat, both paddlers can paddle on the same side opposite that of the wind. By going to "sides" periodically, along with the normal paddling stroke, the tendency of the canoe to turn into the wind can be fought. Another technique is for the stern paddler to use a few J-strokes, or even a rudder if absolutely necessary. These severe corrective strokes should only be used in the most extreme conditions because they slow your speed significantly. A C-1 paddler has little choice but to paddle on the side opposite from the direction of the wind, leaning the boat down to that side. This can become quite exasperating and tiring after a while. Another technique is to paddle a zigzag or "tacking" type of a course. With this method, the C-1 (or even C-2 paddlers) first angle slightly away from the wind, then switch and angle back slightly into the wind. It's obvious you will be paddling a little farther, but you will be able to paddle hard and more importantly, you will be able to paddle on both sides of the canoe using this technique.

As you can see, the various combinations of current, water depth, river width, obstacles, and wind which you encounter in canoe racing are literally endless. No two rivers or lakes are alike and therefore no two race courses are alike. Each one presents its own unique set of challenges. For the sophisticated paddler, there is simply never a dull moment. The more types of race courses you paddle, the better racer you will become. As this happens, you will learn to get every ounce of speed possible out of the conditions you face. Keep working on these water reading skills, and you too will find the fast lanes.

Chapter 7

The Fine Art Of Wake Riding

"I Get By With A Little Help From My Friends"
John Lennon and Paul McCartney

Anyone who has watched the Tour de France cycling race on television is familiar with the technique of drafting. Cyclists, riding one behind the other, cut the drag caused by wind and save up to 20% of the energy needed to maintain a given speed. They take turns "pulling" for each other at the head of the pack and then drop back and ride in the slipstream. Likewise, runners and cross-country skiers also draft, especially when they are battling headwinds.

There is a similar phenomenon in canoe racing. Some call it "drafting," but it's not. It is "wake riding" or "riding wash." The canoes are actually riding or surfing on the waves created by the lead canoe. Next to the basic technique of the racing stroke, there is no skill more critical to master than that of riding wake. It is the ability of racing canoes to ride the waves created by other canoes which causes the real excitement and dynamics of any canoe race.

There are essentially two ways to ride wake — by riding the waves directly behind a canoe or by side waking, riding the wave that is pushed out to either side of a canoe. Let's first take a look at the more common method, riding the stern wake.

Riding The Stern Wake

A sleek racing canoe slicing through still water is fast and efficient but still displaces a lot of water as it moves along, throwing off waves behind and to both sides. Immediately behind the canoe there is a burble of disturbed water, sometimes known as a "hole," and then a wave of energized water rushing in to fill the void created by the moving canoe. This is the stern wake, or backwash, a great source of potential energy for canoe racers to utilize.

Photograph by Inner Mountain

Any racer can benefit from riding the stern wake.

Most experienced racing canoeists have learned the obvious advantages of riding the stern wake of another canoe. They try to place the bow of their boat a foot or two behind the stern of the canoe ahead, situating their canoe on the "downhill" side of the wave formed behind the lead canoe. This causes the stern of their canoe to be picked up on the wave, and they "surf" forward toward the hollow near the stern of the canoe ahead. It's like paddling downhill. You can, by maintaining this position, conserve approximately 10% to 15% of the energy normally required to maintain the pace you're traveling at. That is why it is not unusual to see a whole string of canoes in any big race, one following the other.

Every boat that goes by you gives you a gift of energy — their wake. Even if they are slightly faster than you, if they give you a boost on their wave, you should be able to sit there and not get dropped. Christmas in July!

There are three or four ridable waves behind a canoe, each about a canoe-length apart. They can be visualized as peaks and valleys in the water. The further back you are, the weaker and lower the waves are and the more work it will take to maintain the pace. The trick is to work your way up to the first wave. Experienced paddlers might ride the third wave for a bit, then power ahead to the second wave (you have to climb over the peak until you feel yourself getting a ride on the downhill side), and use the energy in that wave for a while. They then sprint ahead to grab the first wave and ride that. But, it's not as easy as it sounds. When you are new to canoe racing, it is often difficult to feel the stern waves and position your boat to best take advantage of them. Also, in most situations, there's a jumble of stern waves and side waves to sort out. That's why it may be easier, if you can do it, to stay off to the side until you can pull in directly behind the lead canoe. Regardless of how you do it, if you can just keep your canoe behind the lead canoe, you are likely to be able to ride one of the stern waves for a while. If you can no longer ride the wave and get "dropped," try to jump on the next faster boat that passes and grab a ride for as long as you can. That's how you learn.

When moving your canoe forward up and over a canoe wake, be aggressive. Don't try to gradually bull your way over — it takes too much energy. Pop the canoe up and over with a sharp sprint. As soon as you have made it so that your canoe is surfing forward, relax and slow your stroke rate down.

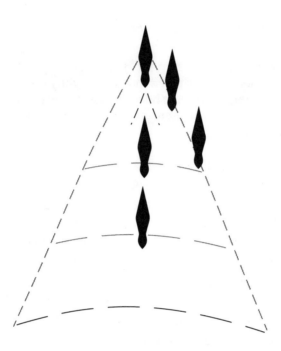

Schematic view of the stern and side wakes off a lead canoe with canoes shown in some of the wake-riding positions.

You will find that you can't just sit there in the perfect spot on the backwash and ride — it takes some work and experience to keep your canoe positioned. You'll tend to drift from side to side, forward and back, and have to make constant corrections. This is particularly true in a C-1 due to the zig-zag path of the lead canoe. It helps to match your strokes and switches with the canoe ahead but you will still find yourself having to periodically use some extra energy to get back on the wake. It is much easier in a C-2. There, the bow paddler, being right up where the action is, can keep on the stern wake by using some draw strokes or by calling the switches.

Wake riding takes practice. If you paddle solo, work with a friend , switching positions from time to time. Practice falling back or drifting off to the side and then sprinting back into position. Tandem partners can likewise practice with another boat.

One thing that makes stern waking more popular with novices then side waking is the tendency of your canoe to seek the hollow in the water behind the the lead boat. This "homing instinct" will help you hang in there when you are drafting a canoe from a stern position. One of the consequences of stern wake riding is inadvertent bumping — it is easy, especially for beginners, to overshoot and bang the stern of the canoe ahead. This can throw the lead canoe off course but, as shown in the excellent video by Mike and Tanna Fries, all it takes is a quick rudder stroke by the stern paddler and the lead canoe is on its way.

Photograph by Dick Mansfield

A "Canoe-Eye" view of the wakes thrown off a C-1.

When going into a headwind, the stern wake is often the place to be. Not only do you get a nice ride, but the lead team helps break the wind. It can also give you some protection from the heavy waves kicked up by the wind.

Disadvantages Of The Stern Wake

For the accomplished paddler, there are some disadvantages to using the stern wake. First, the canoe in front can drop you off the wake easily. The lead canoe just has to suddenly sprint or abruptly change direction and before you know it, you have "fallen off" the wave and are left behind. This situation is exacerbated if you are the

Photograph by Dick Mansfield

C-1 stern waking requires constant attention and corrections.

second or even third canoe in a line of back waking canoes. If the front canoe attacks, you are simply not in a position to respond.

In cycling, riders who continually draft and never pull their share are known by the term, "wheel suckers." These riders have been known to be sprayed with water bottles or even forced off the road. In canoeing, such drafting tactics are met with the same disdain by those who end up "pulling" all the time. Here, the lead canoeists can cause problems for the waking canoeists by splashing them with their paddles and putting water in the follower's boats.

The third drawback to stern waking is that when you enter shallow water, the wave length of the wakes shortens up and following canoes will immediately "fall off" and be unable to stay with the lead boat.

Most of these stern wave disadvantages are addressed by the technique of side waking — a technique that, while more difficult, is favored by most experienced canoe racers. It is something that every serious newcomer to the sport should master. Here's why.

Why The Side Wake?

As any canoe goes through the water, it not only creates waves behind, but also creates waves that are pushed off to either side. These waves go off at an angle behind the moving canoe in the shape of an inverted V, with the canoe at the apex of the V. The side wake stretches out behind the canoe for a substantial distance and is highest very close to the boat and gradually gets smaller as you proceed away from the canoe.

You can enjoy the advantages of riding side wake even though you are over a boat length away from the canoe creating the wake. What are these advantages? First of all, unlike the stern wake situation just described, it is much more difficult to be dropped when side waking. If the lead canoe sprints, the following canoe can simply slide backwards along the side wake or drop in behind and pick up the stern wake. Second, the side waking canoe is not as vulnerable to being splashed or filled with water by the lead canoe. Third, when in shallow water, the side wake is the only viable wake that can be ridden. Fourth, a side waking canoe is in a good position to "attack" and sprint when necessary. Fifth, and most significantly, side waking can be to the mutual advantage of all the canoes which are side waking one another.

The disadvantage of side waking is that it is a bit more difficult to learn. A problem arises because the canoe that is waking will be constantly attracted toward the canoe whose wake is being ridden. If you are on the left side of the lead canoe, your bow will turn toward the right, and vice versa. This can lead to constant bumping when the paddlers are inexperienced.

In a C-2, the way to prevent your canoe from being attracted toward the other canoe is to use a combination of quarter draw strokes from the bow and slightly sweeping strokes in the stern, in essence drawing your bow slightly away from the lead canoe. A more efficient method for keeping either solo or tandem canoes from being attracted toward one another is to roll your canoe away from the other boat. Thus, if you are on the left side of the lead boat, you would roll the right side of your boat down just enough so that it would track in a straight line rather than being pulled to the right.

When side waking very close, where the waking benefits are the greatest but the pull into the other canoe is also the strongest, experienced teams will sometimes paddle "sides" on the inside. This maintains the close proximity and keeps the canoes from bumping.

The best way to learn side wake riding technique is to go out with another boat and practice. It won't take long before sitting on another canoe's side wake becomes as easy to you as sitting on the back wake.

Side Waking Strategies

The ability to ride a side wake opens up a whole new realm of dynamics and strategies which you can add to your canoe racing skills. The optimum place to be while riding side wake is approximately two feet to the left or the right of the leading canoe. You may slide your canoe out along the angled side wake and still feel the surfing action, up to a point over a boat's length away from the lead canoe. In shallow water, move your canoe forward relative to the lead canoe since the wave length of all waves in shallow water tends to shorten and waves move closer together.

Try to ride the wake of a canoe which is faster or at least as fast as your canoe. If a canoe is coming on you from behind, the best way to enter the side wake is to move your canoe close to the passing canoe and allow the side wake to pick up your stern. Once your canoe is up on the side wake, you can relax somewhat and slow your stroke rate down slightly. On the other hand, if you are coming on a canoe from behind, then you must "jump" over the lead canoe's side wake by sprinting out from behind the canoe and punching your canoe up and over the side wake. Again, as soon as you are over the wave, relax and slow your stroke rate down.

The best aspect of riding side wake is that canoes may actually help each other by taking turns "pulling." By mutually agreeing to work with the other canoe or canoes, each boat takes a turn in the lead while the other canoe rides the side wake. By taking turns in this manner, two or more canoes can go faster as a group than a single canoe can alone. Thus, as a group, you may be able to pull away from single canoes following you or catch canoes in front of you. This type of side waking strategy gives rise to the large "packs" of canoes strung together in echelon fashion that one sees at any top pro race.

Photograph by Dick Mansfield

Three canoes in the right foreground maintain optimum side wake distance. Canoe to the left can slide in closer to pick up a better ride. Trailing canoes are moving up to ride stern wakes.

When paddling in a pack of three or more canoes, strategy, tactics, and position all come into play. You will find that canoeists in these packs vary their speed tremendously, going from a slow cruising pace to a sudden sprint. You must constantly watch the other paddlers to be ready so that you do not get dropped off the pack. The arrival of a tight turn, a portage, or a shallow water stretch, is a sure signal for an attack.

If you get dropped from a pack, it is important to quickly redouble your efforts to get back on one of the side wakes. Flopping around in the irregular and criss-crossing waves created behind a pack is frustrating and energy consuming. It is important at that moment to make a strong move to get back with the pack: the alternative will be to drop back out of contention.

Photograph by Inner Mountain

Three elite C-2 teams in "picture-perfect" side waking position.

When trying to catch a pack of canoes or when attempting to get up on the side wake in shallow water, it is usually best to swing wide and jump the side wakes some distance away from the other canoe or canoes, where the side wake is low and easy to cross. Once you are in undisturbed water in front of the side wave, you may slide your canoe over to a better wave-riding position, close to the other canoes. Remember also that when you can keep your canoe even with another canoe, you will <u>both</u> pick up some wave energy from each other. If you let your canoe fall back a few feet, you will get a better ride. Conversely, if you move your canoe forward a few feet, the other canoe will get a better ride.

Photograph by Inner Mountain

Once you are comfortable on the side wake, a whole new dimension of canoeing strategy will be opened to you.

As the finish line approaches, the canoe packs will usually break up. A "grinding" type team which does not have a very fast sprint will want to try to break away from the pack substantially before the finish. A sprinting team will want to ride other canoes until the last possible moment, then attack off the front to victory. (See Chapter 10 for a more detailed discussion of tactics to employ when side waking or finishing a race.)

Side waking is a viable and efficient form of wake riding which is not utilized by most canoeists to its full potential. So whether you are entering your first canoe triathlon or have years of paddling experience, try getting out on the side wake during the race and using that energy to better your position. Once you are comfortable on the side wake, a whole new dimension of canoeing strategy will be opened to you.

Try It, You'll Like It

Waking, whether it be stern waking or side waking, is a legitimate racing technique that can allow you to move your canoe faster through the water with less energy. If you're a newcomer to canoe racing, you will find that wake riding is a great way to recycle the energy of faster paddlers — to use them for as long as possible to move along faster than you can on your own. You can make up some of what you might lack in technique or training through the judicious grabbing of rides off faster boats.

For good canoe racers, waking lets you work with other canoes to improve your overall position relative to others in the race. It also allows you to conserve energy. Most of all, wake riding provides the dynamics and real excitement in canoe racing. The packs will form, and one by one the slower or less fit teams will drop away. When the front runners near the finish line, the fireworks start. Everyone makes their move, and the spectators get to see who has what left.

So learn how to wake ride and practice until you become proficient. You'll get to love every waking moment!

Chapter 8

Shallow Water

"I like the hard water..."
Serge Corbin

When a canoe racing team enters a stretch of shallow water, the stern of the canoe seems to sink and you swear that you are paddling uphill. That's because you are! The canoe slows down, feels heavy and sluggish, and each stroke becomes more exhausting than the next. Welcome to shallow water.

One of the first lessons any canoe racer learns is this: all water is not created equal. Just as running and bicycle racing have their hills and mountains — places where the strongest and fittest athletes leave the competition behind — so canoe racing has its shallow water. These "mountains," while not as visible as those encountered by runners and bike racers, can have the same dramatic impact on a canoe race. Yes, "shallow water effect" gives canoe racing its mountains and provides canoe racers with the ultimate challenge to fitness and technique. Shallow water is where the "tough get going."

No single element in canoe racing makes a greater difference to the ultimate outcome than substantial amounts of shallow water. The disparity between teams which are capable of handling shallow water and those which are not is dramatic. The team that can "pop" the canoe in shallow water will quickly open up vast amounts of distance between themselves and any team that might be following and is unable to handle the shallows. Just as Greg LeMond waits for the Alps or the Pyrenees Mountains to make his move in the Tour De France and in so doing gains big chunks of time over his less fit competitors, so can you look forward to opening up similar gaps on your competition during the shallow stretches of a canoe race.

Handling Shallow Water

Nowhere are the lessons of shallow water brought home to a greater degree than in numerous races in the Midwest and Canada where the late summer rivers are often less than two feet deep. One of the most notoriously difficult shallow water races occurs in the northern reaches of Quebec at a two-day pro stage race held near the town of Mount Laurier. The river there is broad and shallow, often only a foot deep or even less. Any racer who plans to paddle this course in the same way he or she would paddle deep water is in for a long two days of racing. So it was with me when I first went to Mount Laurier during my early years of canoe racing. I thought the way to handle shallow water was simply to move the bow person as far forward as possible and just keep paddling hard. I was wrong.

That particular year at Mount Laurier, the river was very shallow. We're talking two to ten inches of water. You could literally walk across the entire river and never get your calves wet. This was not intermediate water but all-out shallow water — four hours worth and much of it upstream.

Right at the start my partner and I were in trouble. The waves thrown off from our competition were huge. Our boat was thrown around and we continuously seemed to run into huge walls of water which we simply could not get over. My poor bow partner "ate his knees" as he slid his seat as far forward as he could but that did not help. Once we got away from the start, more and more canoes passed us. We finally turned a buoy and began paddling upstream. We just couldn't get our bow down so we tried to stay about ten to fifteen feet from shore, looking for slightly deeper water. Again, canoe after canoe went by us on the <u>inside</u>, paddling in two to five inches of water! By the time we got to the finish line, it was all we could do to keep from finishing dead last. We finally figured out that we must have been doing something wrong. Smart, huh? What we were doing wrong was nearly everything.

Photograph by Dick Mansfield

Serge Corbin (in the bow) and Brett Stockton excel in shallow water.

So how should you handle shallow water? First, let's look at what is actually happening to your canoe. Essentially, as the bottom of the river or lake comes closer to the canoe, the interaction of the hull and the water causes the waves created by the moving canoe to get shorter in wave length. Not only do they get shorter as the water shallows, they also get larger and actually "move forward" relative to the canoe hull. The result is that the major wave upon which your canoe normally rides in deep water gets bigger and moves forward to a location under the front portion of your canoe. Consequently, your bow rides up on the wave and your stern drops. If you continue to paddle with your normal pace and effort, your bow will ride up on the shallow water wave and the stern will tend to sink down, giving you the dreaded "uphill" feeling. You'll work harder but your speed will slow. And other canoe racers who know how to paddle shallow water will leave you in their wakes.

The solution to real shallow water — and by that I mean water less than one foot deep — is to dramatically change your technique and speed. Just as a speedboat gets up and planing, so do you need to get your canoe up and planing — you've got to get your boat speed increased dramatically so you can get and keep your canoe ahead of the shallow water wave. To do this, to get the canoe hull speed maximized, you need an all-out sprint as you enter shallow water. With an all-out effort, you will be able to keep your canoe on the "downside" (in front of) of the shallow water wave. By achieving top hull speed, you can keep the bow wave back to the mid or stern portion of the canoe so the back of your boat will be literally picked up and you will be able to plane or surf forward at a speed which can exceed your speed in deep water. Once you get there, you'll love it.

Photograph by Dick Mansfield

Bob Rapant and Bob MacDowell "pop" their boat in shallow water.

The shallow water sprint requires both paddlers to pick up their efforts, both in terms of the intensity being applied to each stroke and also in terms of stroke rate. You must increase your stroke rate because even though you are giving an all-out effort, you can often put only a few inches of the paddle blade in the water due to the shallowness of the water. You must increase your intensity to the maximum because you need the utmost hull speed to get ahead of the shallow water wave.

> **Whether bringing the canoe up to maximum speed as you enter shallow water, the best solution is explosive acceleration, also known as "jumping" the canoe. A short burst of all-out effort combined with a slightly quicker and shorter stroke rate will enable you to "pop" your canoe from the very beginning of shallow water stretches. It will also allow you to burst through a shallow water wave and let you surf forward on that wave. These explosive sprints can require as little as 10 to 20 seconds of effort but the dividends paid will be well worth the price.**

Another key to shallow water is anticipation. It is by far and away better to anticipate shallow water by popping the canoe up to maximum hull speed <u>before</u> you enter the shallows. In this way, as the wave size increases and wave length shortens, you will be able to get your canoe ahead of and up on the shallow water wave from the beginning. This is much preferable to having to jump over one or more shallow water waves that have built up in front of your canoe. That's why it helps to know where the shallow water stretches come on any race course. But if you are not able to pre-run the course, then another method of anticipation is to be aware that you will probably "feel" the effects of oncoming shallow water before you actually see it. So, as soon as the canoe even hints at getting that "sinking" feeling, jump it up ahead of the shallow water wave before it is too late.

**The best way to learn the technique of "jumping" or
"popping" your canoe in shallow water is to find a
very shallow section of your favorite pond or river
and repeatedly practice. Remember to start off with
short stretches of shallow water at first. Gradually
increase the shallow water stretches as your profi-
ciency increases. You will soon learn that once you
get the boat properly aligned on the shallow water
wave, you can then ease off on your stroke rate and
intensity to a slight degree, allowing the energy of
the wave to help propel you forward.**

Once you experience the thrill of getting a canoe up and planing
in shallow water, it will be a revelation. You will wonder why you
disliked shallow water all this time. The exhilaration of the speed
you can obtain in just a few inches of water will bring you back for
more.

That Dreaded Intermediate Water

If you took a poll among marathon canoe racers as to what water
condition they dislike the most, I'm willing to bet that the vast
majority would answer "cement water." (They might also call it
"intermediate water," "suck water," "junk water," or some other
unkind term which is not printable in this book.) Whether it's called
intermediate water or cement water, the meaning is the same. This
is water which is between one foot and two to three feet in depth.
This type of water is indeed dreaded because it exhibits most of the
drawbacks of shallow water but none of the benefits.

Cement water causes some of the same effects as real shallows.
The wave length of cement water waves shortens a bit and the
waves increase somewhat in size and move slightly forward,
creating that suck down "cement" feeling. But's that where the
similarity stops — the waves created are not sufficiently large to
cause the surfing or planing action that can be experienced in
shallow water. So everyone's canoe, from pro to novice, tends to go
slightly uphill and the going is tough. It takes a lot of effort to keep
the canoe going fast in this water and you get little for it— you can't
get the exhilaration of popping a canoe as you can in shallow water.

Many races, like New York's General Clinton, have many stretches of the dreaded intermediate water. Here, Tanna Fries and Jan Whitaker negotiate such a section.

Don't just accept "cement" water. Watch the other boats, learn from them. Look for shallow water along the shoreline — stick that "wing" of your boat almost on the river bank. If you are lucky, perhaps you can find some real shallows to go in for a welcome respite from the rigors of intermediate water.

Simply put, paddling in cement water is a chore. The going is rough, the going is slow, the boat just never feels like it's moving well. The only practical way to deal with cement water is to just put the hammer down. Go as hard as you can and increase your stroke rate slightly over your normal race pace. You will find that cement water does reward the fittest paddlers but not quite as dramatically as that of real shallows. When in intermediate water, it helps to take consolation in the fact that everyone is in the same boat — a "cement water" boat.

Trimming The Canoe For Shallow Water

Most canoe racers generally agree that shallow water requires the racing canoe to be trimmed substantially bow down. I find that having the bow one inch to one-half inch down will do the trick although there are plenty of racers who prefer to go up to two and a half inches bow down in shallow water. You will have to experiment to find the exact trim you prefer. The important point is that you want to have your boat trimmed properly <u>before</u> you hit the shallow water. If you know the race has a great deal of shallow water, then you should have it trimmed properly to begin with, before the race begins.

> **For races in which you know there will be a predominant amount of shallow water, try utilizing a paddle approximately one inch shorter than usual. A shorter paddle assists in two important ways. First, it facilitates a quicker stroke rate. Second, it helps prevent your upper grip hand from being too high. If you can't get your paddle blade fully immersed in the water due to the shallow bottom, your entire paddle will be higher than normal during the stroke and your upper arm will particularly feel the effects of this new position. A shorter paddle shaft helps prevent this problem. You may also want to use a slightly heavier and stronger paddle, or at least a paddle with a more rugged blade, since you will invariably be hitting rocks, stumps, and whatever else inhabits the shallow water bottom.**

Some bow paddlers spend a great deal of time sliding their seats forward in shallow water. There is nothing inherently wrong with this as long as it is done substantially before you get to shallow water. The problem some teams run into is that inexperienced bow paddlers often start to slide their seat forward too late. They are caught "sliding" when they should be sprinting. Both paddlers need to be paying attention to increasing the hull speed instead of playing around with seats. The "sliding seat delay" usually results in the canoe ending up behind the shallow water wave, with the expected consequences. The bow goes up and the stern down. What must be done then is to expend a great deal of energy trying to get the boat up and going.

Long Stretches of Shallow Water

I know what you're thinking. Sprinting all out to get maximum benefit from shallow water waves is all well and good, but what happens when the shallow water goes on for miles? You can't sprint forever.

True enough. But you will be surprised how far you can go by getting the canoe planing on the shallow water wave and utilizing the energy of that wave. Once the canoe is up and running fast, you will be able to back off on your intensity and stroke rate, while still keeping the canoe screaming forward. This is why the fittest paddlers invariably dominate in shallow water.

Photograph by Tricia Heed

A mixed team working hard to keep the boat on a shallow water wave.

A technique that is successful for many racers in shallow water is to drop the lower hand (the hand grasping the shaft) close to the paddle blade, if it is not there already. This lowering of the hand, even an inch or two, will provide increased leverage and purchase in shallow water. This lower hand position also assists in increasing stroke rate and improving accuracy in the "catch" phase of the stroke. This will help you increase your acceleration in sprints.

The General Clinton, the AuSable marathon, and Mt. Laurier have miles and miles of shallow water. They also have both been dominated in recent years by one man, Serge Corbin. Paddling with a variety of partners, he has proven to be just about unbeatable on these courses. Why? Because he also happens to be the world's best shallow water paddler. When the going gets tough, he goes.

Even after successfully getting up on the shallow water wave and backing off on your effort slightly, you will find that you cannot keep this pace up for more than a few minutes. The level of energy required to keep your canoe planing is too great. Once you fall back off the wave, your best alternative is to maintain your stroke rate slightly higher than usual with a shorter, crisper power phase. Then hammer forward as fast as your fitness level will allow. The higher the speed you are able to maintain, the more the shallow water effect will be minimized. Also keep in mind that everything you do is relative to what other paddlers are doing. If you are having trouble with long stretches of shallow water, fear not, so will everyone else. The team that can go the hardest the longest is going to come out on top.

Many teams actually look forward to long shallow water races. In deep water courses, large packs will form and it is difficult for the better paddlers to drop the less fit paddlers. But when shallow water stretches are lengthy, packs will break up and the fittest and fastest paddlers will invariably be in the lead at the end.

Wake Riding In Shallow Water

Shallow water causes major difficulties for wake riding canoes. Because of the shortened wave length and larger wave size, it is nearly impossible to properly ride wake. This is particularly true of the stern wake — if you are back on the stern wake, you will find that with the shortened waves, it is nearly impossible to find a wave you can ride. You continuously feel as if you are plowing into the wave in front of you and being forced into the uphill position.

Side waking presents some possibilities although, because of the large size of the wake, you can encounter some severe control problems. It's not uncommon to see canoes end up sideways on a big wake or beached up on the shore. When trying to ride on the side wake in shallow water, slide your wake-riding canoe slightly away from the other canoe and backwards on the side wake, finding a position where the wave size is not so huge. This will reduce control problems and help your canoe from being shot sideways.

> **If you are behind other canoes in shallow water, try to move ten to twenty feet on either side of the lead boat. The waves here are more easily handled and it is also a simpler chore to control the boat and move forward or backward relative to the other canoes.**

Because of the difficulties inherent with waking in shallow water, the best solution is to be the lead boat. If you can get to shallow water first, you are going to cause the waking canoes a great deal of problems. This is why upcoming stretches of shallow water invariably cause massive sprints.

Jumping Shallow Water Waves

You are certainly not always going to be the lead boat in shallow water. Nor are you always going to be able to get in front of the shallow water wave. What do you do then when confronted with what looks to be a wall of water in front of your bow? When behind a large shallow water wave, the first thing to remember is what not to do: do not simply slug forward at 80-90% effort, continuously driving your bow up into the wave, causing your canoe to take an even more exaggerated stern down position. The proper strategy is either to let the canoe slide back so that the stern is picked up by the next wave from behind, or better yet, get over the wave in front.

This has to be done quickly. Laboring along with your bow riding high up on a shallow water wave is exhausting and ineffective.

The first option to consider is getting over the wave so that you can place your canoe on the front portion — the downhill portion — of the wave. This will enable you to reap the benefits of all that energy. Jumping a wave requires total commitment by both paddlers to an all-out, explosive sprint. The canoe needs to be accelerated quickly so that it can be jumped up and over the wave. If you are not successful in getting over the wave within ten or fifteen seconds, then drop back, rest, and try again.

Practice "jumps" during training. That is, practice accelerating the canoe to maximum speed from a normal race pace within a period of a few seconds and hold that maximum speed for up to 20 seconds.

The second option to consider is to slide your canoe farther away from the canoe that is creating the wave. In doing this, the wave will gradually lessen in height, and you should be able to find a point at which your boat speed will allow you to jump it. If you are not able to get over the wave at any location, then simply let your canoe drop back until your stern is picked up by the next following wave. Ride this wave until you have rested, and then attack again.

Remember that if you are going to jump up and over a wave, do so with maximum speed, acceleration, and commitment. You should only have to sustain this level of energy output for a few seconds to successfully put the wave behind you.

Paddle "Poling"

In water that is extremely shallow — that is less than four to five inches deep — many experienced racers are able to utilize their paddles effectively in a "poling" technique. In this procedure, both racers actually drive their paddle blades into the bottom of the river or lake and push the boat forward with a downward action of the upper arm. Naturally, this technique usually requires a relatively sandy bottom. It also requires both paddlers to work together. The stroke rate must be slowed down substantially. Yet in comparison to paddlers who are flailing away with their paddles in just a few inches of water, this technique can be surprisingly fast.

Don't try this for the first time in a race — first find a sandy bottom river and practice. Improper coordination between bow and stern partner can end with a quick dip and an overturned canoe. Recovery will obviously not be a problem in two or three inches of water but any spill should be avoided at all costs.

C-1 And Shallow Water

Modern C-1 canoes react similarly to their C-2 brethren in shallow water. The difference is that the power plant is reduced by half. With only one paddler, it is difficult, if not often impossible, to produce the same levels of acceleration and boat speed as found in a C-2. This makes planing the canoe up in shallow water somewhat more difficult.

All of the normal rules of shallow water paddling apply to the C-1 paddler. When the going gets tougher, the fitter and faster C-1 paddlers will be rewarded admirably. Anticipate shallow water and increase your stroke rate and your speed, just as you would in a C-2. You'll find that the C-1 boat will still jump for you in shallows if you work hard. One word of caution: be conscious of the larger shallow water waves — they can easily flip to a C-1 due to their height and severity.

Weight And The Shallow Water Paddler

It is a common misconception that you have to be a light team in order to paddle fast in shallow water. While being lightweight clearly has certain advantages in shallow water, it is just as clearly not a necessity. Bruce Barton, Serge Corbin, Al Rudquist, Tim Triebold and Mike Fries are all superb shallow water paddlers. None of them are lightweights — the reason they are fast in shallow water is because they exhibit tremendous technique and sprint speed and are therefore able to quickly accelerate their canoes to maximum possible hull speed. Dieting is not the answer to shallow water. Explosive and sustainable speed is.

Basic Shallow Water Strategy Considerations

A general rule for shallow water is, "be fast, be first." Since the first canoe into any shallow water stretch enjoys numerous advantages, it's easy to see why there will be massive sprints before each of these sections. If you can anticipate the shallow water portions of the river so that you can get a jump on your competitors, once you are in the shallow water they will have great difficulty in passing you. When leading, you can make things tough on trailing canoes where the water is less than a foot deep because the waves and holes created behind the stern of your boat will actually leave little water for the following canoe. Often the second canoe will actually be beached and have to wait a few moments before it can again get underway. When you find yourself as the following canoe, keep this in mind, and slide out on the side wake to the left or right of the lead boat.

Any sharp turn in the river provides great opportunities to utilize the shallow water that normally lurks there. If you are the inside team, (the team closest to shore) a sprint going into a shallow water corner can easily drop stern waking canoes. The huge side wake thrown up by your boat can also cause real problems for a canoe that is on your outside side wake. If a canoe is on your inside side wake, a hard sprint will increase your wake to such an extent that the inside boat will have difficulty preventing being turned sideways and driven into shore.

If you happen to find yourself outside a canoe which is sprinting into a corner, allow your canoe to slide out and back slightly on the side wake. Both you and your partner need to be alert to prevent their wave from throwing your boat sideways. A slight draw or quarter draw stroke from both paddlers will often do the trick. Also try rolling the canoe so that the inside gunnel (the one nearest the lead boat) is up. This will help prevent being shot off at an angle.

If you find yourself on the inside, but on the lead boat's side wave, an upcoming corner provides a bright opportunity to put the hammer down. The huge shallow water side wave thrown off by your sprinting canoe may enable you to cause control problems for the lead boat and their side wake will also allow you to potentially

Photograph by Dick Mansfield

Mike Fries (bow) and Tim Triebold (stern) find the best
line through a technical shallow water section.

sling-shot into the lead. If you are not able to sprint by the lead boat
then you need to be doubly aware of the potential for getting thrown
into shore by the increasingly large side wake thrown by the lead
boat. In this case, it is often best for the bow paddler to be drawing
toward the lead canoe (away from shore) while the stern paddler is
paddling hard on the shore side of the canoe. It is also of some
assistance here to roll the canoe slightly so the shore side gunnel is
down. These techniques will help you from ending up with your
canoe up on shore like a beached whale.

If you are leading a pack of canoes going into any stretch of
shallow water, be sure to stay there. Hit it first and hit it hard. Make
the waking canoes work and maybe you will drop one or two of
them. If a competitor gets the jump on you and gets by, stay in the
side wake. Slide out away if you have to, but try not to get dropped.

On the other hand, if you are in a waking (following) canoe and
coming into shallow water, think about attacking first and getting

by the lead boat. If that isn't possible, find the best side wave available, and stay as close as possible. As soon as the lead canoes slow down, jump right back up on a good wave.

The moral of all this is that shallow water can be both fun and fast. Shallow water can make or break you in most canoe races. But don't let shallow water get you down, look at it as an opportunity to put distance between you and the competition. Train in shallow water, even though it takes more effort. Work to improve your acceleration, your boat speed, and your overall fitness. These will be the tools that you can utilize to get your boat up and on the right side of those shallow water waves to leave your competition behind. Get it down pat and you'll never dread those huge shallow water waves again.

Chapter 9

PORTAGING

"These guys don't just portage — They fly!"
Spectator at the Boulevard Portage — Classique International de Canots

It is one of the great ironies in both marathon and downriver canoe racing that some of the most crucial moments of any race occur when the participants are not paddling, but carrying their canoes overland. You have trained for months to turn your upper torso into a cardiovascular paddling machine, and now you must suddenly get out of your canoe, pick it up, put your legs in gear, and run! Instead of your canoe carrying you through the water, you must now carry it. This can be role reversal of the most dreaded kind.

Not only is portaging something which seems to run counter to all you have trained for, but potential disaster lurks at every point in a portage. For a team which is not conversant with all of the diverse skills involved in portaging, the results can be ruinous. Much more can go wrong during a portage than can go right.

Compounding this irony is the fact that, whenever it occurs, any portage is so important — it nearly always has a dramatic impact on the outcome of a race. A team which may have been leading a race on the water but which is not a competent portaging duo, can easily be caught or passed on the run by less talented paddlers. The

gap that can be opened up on even a short portage is often large
enough so that it is difficult to close, or may not be able to be closed
at all, once back in the water. Any good racer will tell you that there
are few moments in canoe racing as frustrating as working hard to
catch or ride the wake of a fast pack of canoes, only to be
unceremoniously dropped due a bad portage — never to enjoy
those friendly wakes again.

Courtesy Le Nouvelliste

Shades of the Tour de France! Pro racers run the gauntlet of fans at
the Grand Mere portage of the Classique International de Canots.

Portaging has always been a traditional part of canoeing. From the Indians and early explorers, to the westward moving settlers and frontier people, the necessity for portaging one's canoe around dangerous rapids, canyons, waterfalls, and other hazards, has always been there. Indeed, one of the unique aspects of this most special of watercraft is the relative ease with which it may be carried overland by one or two people.

The canoes are lighter now, but the problem remains the same. There are still many rapids and waterfalls to be portaged around. More likely, the hazard will be a man-made one, such as a dam. On some occasions racers must even portage simply because the race organizers have decided it would be a good idea. Organizers recognize that a portage is a chance for spectators to see frenzied action on an up-close and personal basis. For this reason, portages are usually the most popular spot for spectators along any race course. There is nothing fans like better than to watch canoe racers jockey for position as they come to a portage, with canoes bumping, paddles dropping, competitors jumping into the water, and on some occasions flipping over.

Photograph by Tricia Heed

Portages are popular spectator spots along any race course. Here, Bob Zaveral and Brett Stockton run down the famous Boulevard portage in Shawinigan, Quebec during the Classique International de Canots.

The Canoe As The Great Equalizer

While you may have decided to get into canoe racing in the first place for the simple reason that you are not a good runner, don't get discouraged by portages. Even if running is not your strong suit, take heart. Remember, this is not running in its pure sense — it is running with a canoe, and there is a significant difference. Somehow the awkwardness of carrying a canoe on the run greatly lessens the difference between the fastest and the slowest. It is this awkwardness, created by the fact that the canoe must be carried, which minimizes the biomechanical advantage of superior runners.

Preparation is the key to fast portaging. Any properly trained team can portage quickly and efficiently, whether or not they are fast runners. The way to a fast portage is through smoothness, efficiency, and teamwork, and this comes only with practice.

Another factor to consider is that a portage is much more than running. Any portage consists of <u>five distinct elements</u> — only one of which is running. These elements are:

> The approach to the portage
> Getting out of the canoe
> Running with the canoe
> Getting into the canoe
> Getting underway again.

Running fast and efficiently with a canoe depends more on smoothness, teamwork, and the way the canoe is carried than it does on foot speed. While it is certainly true that a pair of especially gifted runners such as Cindy Lynch and Eric McNett, when teamed up and prepared, can make up significant time on a long portage, it is equally true that runners without blinding speed, like an Al Rudquist or a Mike Fries, give very little away to any team while portaging.

If you are a fast runner, then you want to be sure that your portaging skills are honed so that you can maximize every possible advantage from your foot speed. On the other hand, if you are an average or slow runner, you want to pay particular attention to mastering <u>all</u> of the portaging skills. This means, for example, if you can't run fast, you want to be absolutely sure that your transitions are smooth and that you carry the canoe comfortably and without awkwardness. By doing so, you will portage efficiently and you will squeeze every ounce of speed available from your body. For slower runners, it becomes particularly critical to master the four components of portaging which do not include running. These are the areas where disaster can most easily strike and these are the areas where a well-practiced portaging team, whatever their foot speed, can gain competitive advantage.

Portage As Transition

It is particularly important to recognize that any portage is, in essence, a series of complex <u>transitions</u>. These transitions include getting to the portage from the main course in the river or lake in proper position; getting out of the canoe without flipping over, filling the boat, swimming, or losing a partner; getting the boat on the shoulders and beginning to run without dropping paddles, water jugs, or other equipment; getting back in the boat at the end of the portage, again without flipping over or taking on water; and getting underway as fast as possible — all without going into cardiac arrest. In between those transitions, you must run with your boat and all of your gear, perhaps for only a few yards, or possibly for over a mile. Despite the complex skills that all of these numerous transitions involve, too few racers pay heed to this important area of their training. The result is often the waste of a fine paddling effort.

> **C-2 canoes are normally portaged in one of two positions: either right side up, or upside down. The usual method is right side up, as the advance preparation for this technique is not as complicated. Many teams, particularly teams in the 3 X 27 pro class, will prefer to carry their canoe upside down. This is because the canoe can be set up with portage pads on the bow and stern to facilitate comfort and reduce awkwardness. Either method can be equally effective, but when the option is available, particularly on long portages, upside down is often the way to go.**

Setting Up The Boat To Portage

Whether right side up or upside down, the canoe must be prepared properly. When getting a canoe ready to portage in a right side up manner, the most important concern is to be sure that paddles, jugs, food holders, life jackets, and other equipment are securely stowed in the canoe so that they do not fall out or slide around loose. There are few things more annoying than trying to portage with a drink jug flopping around in the canoe, constantly changing the weight distribution and at the same time draining out its precious liquid.

Right Side Up Portaging

As we discussed earlier in the equipment chapter, food and drink jugs should be secured in holders, usually made out of a rigid foam type product, which are normally glued to the canoe. The types of holders are as diverse as the paddlers who create them. If it keeps your jug upright and prevents it from getting loose in the boat while you exit, run, and get in, then it will do. Many paddlers in shorter races which do not involve jug exchanges, simply duct tape their jug to any convenient thwart, foot brace or seat support.

Life jackets can be stowed underneath seats, or wedged in the bow or stern. Although experienced racers sometimes duct tape their life jackets into the boat, this practice is not recommended for obvious safety reasons.

The biggest problem encountered is what to do with your paddle. The spare paddle or paddles should already be secured to the canoe by duct tape or a permanent holder. The problem is with the paddle you are utilizing in the race. Some people portage while carrying their paddle in the off-hand. This method is acceptable for short portages, but it is much more efficient to leave the paddle in the boat on any portage of a hundred yards or more. But where? Often a paddle can be wedged lightly underneath the seat, or foot brace. The paddle should be wedged tight enough so that it will not pop out inadvertently, but not so tight that you risk breakage. Another method is to attach the loose paddle to a clip or holder which has been created for that purpose. Broom handle clips secured to a thwart with a screw do the trick quite nicely.

Photograph by Dick Mansfield

In difficult portages, some racers prefer to carry the paddle
in their off-hand while others wedge it in the canoe.

Upside Down Portaging

Setting up a canoe to portage upside down takes a bit more
planning. The first problem that has to be dealt with is preventing
paddles, life jackets, and other gear from falling out of the canoe
when it is turned upside down. The problem is not as difficult as it
may first appear, especially since most 3 X 27 pro boats are
covered. In nearly all races, there will be a center cover on the pro
canoe, and in big water races the canoe will additionally have a bow
cover and perhaps even a stern cover. Spare paddles and life jackets
can be secured or wedged underneath the covers, which will also
help prevent their falling out when the canoe is flipped over. The
same sort of paddle holders, whether made from broom handle clips
or rigid foam, which are used to portage when going right side up
will work here.

The trickier problem is what to do with the paddles that you are actually using. Most teams solve this problem easily enough by stretching a shock cord across the covered portion of the center of the canoe. When coming into a portage, the paddle blade is wedged underneath the shock cord and the handle is secured to broom handle clips or some similar locking devices which are attached to the top portion of the thwart just behind the bow paddler and just in front of the stern paddler.

The problem of what to do with one's drinking jug while portaging upside down requires a bit more creativity. The easiest and often best solution is simply to jettison the drink jugs at the beginning of an upside down portage, taking on new drink jugs from a pit team at the put-in. In this way, the boat is as light as possible, and the team will have a fresh cold jug of fluid waiting after a tough exertion. This is the method preferred by most pro teams on any portage of substantial length. For shorter portages, and especially where it is difficult to get a pit at the put-in, many teams simply portage right side up and not worry about the jug problem. One of the beauties of having a canoe set up to carry upside down is that it gives you the option of portaging either way, according to the conditions you face.

An amateur cruiser may be set up for upside down portaging in a similar fashion. The missing element is the cover, and this fact requires that a bit more thought be given to the set up. A shock cord across the middle thwart, with broom handle holders screwed to the thwarts behind the bow paddler and in front of the stern paddler takes care of the loose paddle problem. All other items simply have to be extra secure to prevent them from dropping out. The issue as to whether or not to carry jugs and how to keep them in while upside down is solved in the same fashion as with a 3 X 27 pro boat.

Go For Comfort
When portaging upside down, comfort can be maximized by padding the bow and the stern of the canoe. Soft ethafoam pads, similar to the padding used on the canoe seats, can either be contact-cemented or duct-taped to the bow and stern decks. If your canoe

does not have decks sufficiently large to support the pad, it is a simple matter to create such a deck utilizing any light and stiff material such as rigid foam or a thin piece of plastic or wood.

One of the advantageous aspects about portaging upside down is that it provides both bow and stern paddler with various hand position options. If you're in front, once the padded bow is resting on your shoulder, you can either reach up to hold the bottom of the boat, or slide your hand down to grasp the front portion of the bow. A loop of webbing or rope attached to the front-most portion of the gunnel, can also be held to maintain a low hand and arm position.

Photograph by Tricia Heed

Carrying the boat upside down provides numerous hand-hold positions.

The stern paddler has the same two options: holding onto the bottom of the boat for a high arm position, or if a strap is placed across the gunnels eight inches to a foot in front of the stern deck, grasping this lower support. Another way for the stern person to portage is to pad the gunnels and stern deck in a "U-shape," creating the equivalent of a small portage yoke. Then you can actually rest the canoe upside down squarely on both shoulders with your head up in the canoe. This has the advantage of keeping the canoe well balanced and stable. You can reach up and hold the bottom of the canoe, hold the gunnel, or even let your arm hang on the supports under the rear seat. However, from this position, all the stern paddler can see are the wet footprints of the bow paddler!

The Portage Approach

All portages begin long before the boats are pulled out of the water. When you are within several minutes of an upcoming portage, the first thing to keep in mind is to fight the natural urge to get overexcited. Keep a cool head and communicate with your partner. It does not hurt to verbally review the upcoming portage and the particular unique aspects of that portage with your partner as you approach.

You should then begin to loosen, bend, and pump your legs, so they will not be so stiff once on dry land. This is particularly critical for the bow person whose legs may have been crammed and jammed for a lengthy period of time. Do not hesitate to slide the seat back momentarily and really get the blood flowing.

Since it is an advantage to be first to a portage, you should always be aware of your boat position. Sprints are the order of the day when any portage is approached. So if you are with other canoes, try to get the jump on the sprint and maintain the best position possible into the take-out, relative to the other canoes. If you are not the fastest boat in your pack and cannot dictate the pace, then consider making every effort to ride the side wake or stern wake of the fastest boat into the take-out. This way, you should be able to arrive at the portage at nearly the same time as the front-runners and be able to expend slightly less energy doing it. Combine this with a swift and efficient take-out and you may be able to beat the lead boat to the portage trail. Naturally, if you are not with a group, there will be no need to change your pace during the approach.

Next, thought has to be given to the nature of the take-out. If you know that the bottom is shallow and sandy, then you can paddle straight in with both paddlers jumping out at approximately the same time. If the take-out is rocky and/or deep, a sideways approach is dictated so that the bow will not be smashed into the rocks, and the stern person will not have to jump out into chest-deep water. A quick post or high brace by the bow person in conjunction with a simultaneous sweep and/draw from the stern person within the last few yards should bring your canoe in sideways with little effort.

The paddles you are using must be stowed at the last moment, unless the portage is so short that you will be able to carry the paddle in your off-hand. On the usual approach, the bow person is able to put the paddle away first, while the stern person gets in one or two final strokes to set the boat up properly. Always be sure your paddles are stowed several yards from shore — there's no advantage to throw in a few last second sprint strokes only to have to slam on the brakes and fumble with your paddle, while your competitors calmly go by.

If you intend to get rid of your jugs so that you are running as empty as possible, they should be thrown out just prior to the final approach, or possibly left to drop out by themselves if you are going to portage upside down. And if you are portaging right side up, don't forget to open the bailer just prior to the take out so that you can drain unwanted water while on the run.

Getting Out

More canoe teams make mistakes while getting out than at any other time during a portage. If you have been paddling for more than an hour or so, your legs will be stiff. The footing is likely to be poor. The excitement of the moment will be high. This is a volatile mix. The best way to avoid problems is with a calm and methodical approach to getting out of your canoe. Run through a mental checklist and try to follow the same procedure at every portage.

If the take-out area is relatively shallow and the bottom is sandy, you will probably come directly into the portage and both bow and stern paddlers can exit the canoe at roughly the same time. I find it best to put one or both of your hands on the gunnels as you swing your legs out of the canoe. This method gives you support and already places your hands on the boat. Keep them there! A big mistake that many paddlers make is to let go of the canoe as they get out and then try to grab the carrying thwarts or straps in either the front of the back. By letting go of the canoe, the boat immediately becomes unsteady and the likelihood of a dump increases. Moreover, you may easily miss when you lunge for the bow or stern. It is far better to lift the canoe by the gunnel or a portion of the seat support which is right next to your body. Both paddlers should then try to swing the boat up to their shoulder in one smooth motion as they exit the water.

Photograph by Michael Moore

Keep your hands on the boat during the takeout until you can swing it up on your shoulders. (Note drink jug and paddle setup on this 3 X 27 pro boat.)

If the approach is rocky and deep, you will be arriving in a sideways position and both paddlers are going to need to get out from the same side — the shallow water side. The same rules apply with regard to grasping the canoe near where you sit and swinging it up to the shoulders smoothly. Bow paddlers, if able to get out first, should not under any circumstance simply pick up the bow and take off. This is the telltale and oft repeated mistake of a novice team. The result is to dump the stern person out of the canoe, simultaneously filling the boat with water. Attempting to gain a millisecond, the bow person ends up costing the team a minute or more.

If the portage take-out is extremely deep so that it does not permit standing in the water, it becomes critically important that both paddlers get out onto the dock or the embankment at the same time. Once you have the canoe parallel to shore and are both out, turn back and lift the canoe up out of the water at the same time. You can then stand, shoulder the canoe, and take off.

> **Remember that being overly excited at the take-out will only cause you to make massive errors. Paddlers will end up in the water, paddles will end up falling, or you may end up carrying a boatload of water across the portage. None of these possibilities fosters a fast portage.**

Next time you have the opportunity to watch a top team portage, take careful note. You will see that the take-out is handled in a methodical, almost mechanical, fashion. Once both paddlers are out of the water and the boat is on the shoulders, then the racers take off at full speed.

Running With The Canoe

Once you are up on dry land, and the canoe is comfortably on your shoulders, then run as fast as you can while staying within your aerobic capabilities. You must strike a balance between running as rapidly as possible without going into such oxygen debt that you will not be able to paddle fast once you put back in.

As quickly as possible, attempt to settle into a pace which both paddlers are comfortable with. Teamwork and communication are key. The need to communicate is particularly critical for the stern person, who is observing the bow person and attempting to match the pace. If the pace is too fast, too slow, or just right, it's important for the stern person to let the bow person know. Things will go smoother if the stern paddler can synchronize the striking of the right foot with the left of the bow person, or vice versa. Another method is to attempt to have both paddler's left (or right) feet striking simultaneously. Depending on relative stride length, one of these two approaches will result in a smooth feeling portage style.

From the beginning of a portage to the end of a portage, keep at least one hand on your canoe. Before your feet hit the water, at least one of your hands should be grasping the gunnel, a seat support, or the seat itself. Lift the canoe to your shoulder in one smooth motion. At the put-in, simply reverse the procedure. Keeping a hand on the boat at all times will eliminate major problems at both the take-out and the put-in.

In carrying the canoe, it is imperative that it be held as directly upright as possible. The best way to do this is to lean the boat slightly in toward your head. This will create a comfortable pocket formed by your shoulder and side of your head in which the canoe may sit. It has the added benefit of allowing your upper arm, which is holding onto the gunnel, to hang in a more relaxed position. If the boat starts to roll significantly away from your head, you will in effect have to push the boat up with your outside arm. This will exhaust you quickly, and will slow your running speed in dramatic fashion.

Most teams also find that it is least awkward to carry the canoe on opposite shoulders, that is, if the bow person has the boat on the left shoulder, the stern person should be carrying it on the right. This is a general rule, but is not hard and fast. Many teams portage with the boat riding on the same shoulder. This is fine, so long as both paddlers consciously keep the boat snug against the sides of their head, thus enabling their outside arms to hang lightly on the canoe. Once the boat rolls away from the shoulder and head, the portage will go from being slightly unpleasant to agony, and portage speed will suffer accordingly.

While running with the canoe, particularly on a lengthy portage, most paddlers will shift the canoe from shoulder to shoulder every so often. This is best handled by one or the other paddler calling a "hut," just as in the water.

A simple but significant concept to keep in mind is the fact that most portages naturally begin with an uphill climb out of the river or lake. During this initial stage of the portage, it is best to keep a conservative pace. Your feet will be wet and legs stiff, so accelerate slowly. Once you have proceeded for a distance and have found your running legs, the pace can be increased. When the hill is crested and you begin the usual downhill descent to the put-in, both paddlers should "let it out."

Courtesy Le Nouvelliste

Al Rudquist and Tim Triebold show how to portage fast over rough terrain as they carry their boat upright.

If you overtake a slower team on the portage trail, yell "track" or some similar warning, and go on by. When you do pass, do so decisively — two canoes side-by-side take up a lot of room. It will be in your own best interest from both a position and psychological standpoint to pass quickly. If you are the slower team, you must not impede a faster team trying to get by you. But you also don't have to run into the trees on a narrow trail; the team behind will have to wait for the appropriate spot to pass. If a team does go by, try to use them as incentive to pick up your own pace.

Photograph by Dick Mansfield

On a downward approach to the put-in, try to keep the boat level.

Getting In

Like the take-out, the put-in at the end of a portage is a spot where disaster lurks. You are tired, your lungs are screaming, your heart is pounding out of your chest, and all you want to do is sit back down in that canoe and begin paddling again. As before, you must resist the temptation to jump wildly into the canoe. I have seen novice canoe racers literally belly flop head-first into their race boats in an ill-conceived attempt to save a few seconds. The end result is usually a quick flip, a cold swim, and a long process of emptying the boat out before getting underway.

If there are several put-in options at portage's end, it is usually best to take the option farthest down the course. If a canoe is putting in right in front of you, try to place your canoe, if possible, in front of this canoe (down the course) so that even if the team gets started first, you have a chance of jumping on the wake as they come by. If you put your canoe behind, and the team takes off, you will be dropped off the wave, and have to grind back on your own.

Once to the water's edge, revert to a methodical and calm entry procedure. Get the boat down smoothly and gently, with both paddlers putting their ends of the canoe down at the same time. It is often best for one paddler, usually the bow paddler, to get in first, while the other paddler steadies the boat. The bow paddler can then begin drawing the bow out into the course, as the stern paddler gets settled. If you're in the bow, don't simply take off as soon as you are seated. If you do, you will more than likely end up paddling C-1 rather than C-2, as your stern person will be left back in the water, or on the rocks.

When getting in where the water is shallow, both paddlers should either straddle the canoe, sit, and swing legs in, or sit down with both legs on the same side, followed with a quick swing of the legs up into position. If the water is deep, hold the gunnels and, with one foot, step carefully into the center of the canoe in the area directly in front of the seat. Sit down, swing the other leg in, and go.

It is darn tempting to take it easy for awhile, waiting for the heart rate to drop and the lungs to come back to you. Resist this temptation. Take advantage. Attack! If you are trying to drop a team, the put-in is a great place to do it. Likewise, if you are trying to catch a team, it is a good idea to try to jump their stern waves and move up at the same time. Attacking while other teams might be expected to be taking it easy is the ideal way to make significant gains.

Photograph by Michael Moore

For short C-1 portages, just grab a gunnel and run.

Getting Underway

As soon as both paddlers are seated with paddles in hand, get underway immediately. Again, it is usually best to leave the portage with the bow racer paddling on the deep water side and the stern racer paddling on the shallow side of the canoe. This will get your canoe angled out into the current in the most efficient manner.

At put-in, try to jump into the fastest paddling pace possible. This is often a place where canoe racers who are out of breath take a short break to recover during the first several hundred yards away from a portage.

Getting underway is not the time to be adjusting drink jugs, eating, or attaching feeding tubes. Wait until you are away from the portage and the hull is back up to top cruising speed. Don't go for the drink tube until you have gotten that boat off your wake, or until you have caught the wave of the boat in front of you. Once things have settled down, then put your drink tube in order, arrange your food, or handle any other "housekeeping" tasks which might present themselves.

C-1 Portaging

The basic concepts of portaging a C-2 apply equally to a C-1, yet there are naturally a few technical differences which cannot be neglected. Clearly you are now down to one person who must somehow carry a 17' to 18'6" canoe with efficiency — a chore most C-2 paddlers find difficult.

For the shortest of portages, it is possible to simply grab a gunnel at the midpoint and run with the canoe in one hand while your paddle is in the other. On portages of any length at all the paddle has to be stowed, and the boat must go to the shoulder. Some C-1 racers have had success by flipping the boat completely over, running with their head up inside. This technique is difficult because the seat set up on most C-1's hinders a comfortable and balanced position. The best approach is to carry the C-1 upright on one shoulder, with the midpoint of the bottom of the canoe resting on the shoulder. It should be angled 45° or so away from you, so that the hard chine tucks in above your elbow (see photo).

Photograph by Dick Mansfield

Excellent C-1 carrying technique for longer portages.

You can switch sides simply by ducking your head and rolling the C-1 across to the opposite shoulder. This technique also helps in dealing with a C-1 portage's greatest enemy—wind. As much as possible, keep the bottom of the canoe (not the open side) into the wind.

Practice, Practice, Practice

All things said and done, only constant practice will turn you into a swift and efficient portager. Make a habit of running a portage during most of your workouts. Find a nice beach and practice approaching, taking-out, running, putting-in, and getting underway. Then paddle a loop and do it again and again until all the transitions become second nature to you.

While it clearly does not hurt to be a fast runner when it comes to portaging, in the final analysis the team that makes the fewest mistakes and which exhibits the most methodical and efficient approach will be the fastest on the portage trail. If you adopt the methods we have outlined, you will soon find that you are looking forward to portages. They will become places of opportunity rather than places of dread.

Chapter 10

RACE STRATEGY AND TACTICS

"There is a time to go fast and a time to go slow."
Gene Jensen

Once you pull together all of the mechanics of canoe racing covered in the previous chapters: technical skills, waking skills, and water reading skills, there is still one missing ingredient to becoming an accomplished competitor. You also need to develop a sophisticated approach to race strategy and tactics. You do this by applying what you have learned and practiced to the ever-changing situations that develop in every race. There are no set plays, no coach to send instructions from the bench. You must make your decisions as you go and react to the situations which develop. This is where the chess game and the fun of canoe racing plays itself out.

Race Day Preparation

Your race day preparation should begin soon after arising in the morning with a nutritious carbohydrate-heavy breakfast that will sit well with your digestive system. This meal should come at least 2-1/2 to 3 hours before the race. Beyond the fact that this meal should be carbohydrate-rich, the precise makeup is not critical. What is important is that you eat food that you are used to — food which you are confident will sit well in your nervous stomach.

You need to consider the clothing you will be wearing, making sure you are prepared for any sudden weather changes that might occur. I know that most experienced canoe racers never go to a race, even in the height of summer, without a polypropylene-type shirt and some warm tights. A quickly moving thunderstorm and cold front can ruin your whole day — and your race — if you have nothing but a cotton T-shirt and gym shorts available.

Double-check all of your equipment, making sure that everything is ready to race. Do you have the seats, foot braces, and foot straps set up properly? Are all drink jugs set and ready to go? Do you have the right length paddles for the course you will be racing? Are life jackets present and accounted for? Do you have plenty of duct tape for those last minute emergencies? Is your tool kit in the car in case something goes wrong during final preparation at the race site?

Get to the race site early and register promptly, putting as many of the little mundane items behind you as quickly as possible so you can concentrate on the task at hand. Get your numbers on your canoe, the drinking system connected, the life jackets in the boat. Pre-race stretching is a must and whether you do it at home, or at the site just prior to the race, I strongly recommend a regimen of stretching exercises which focus on the back, shoulders, neck and arms. Be sure to warm up the muscles beforehand.

It is a good time, while you are going through your stretching regimen, to begin to focus your mental energies. Visualize yourself on the starting line and create a mental picture of you and your partner sprinting to the front or perhaps riding the wave of a favorite's canoe. Think of your paddling technique and try to concentrate on seeing yourself going through all phases of the perfect paddling stroke.

As the start of the race nears, it is absolutely critical that you warm up properly. Some racers like to go for a short jog before getting into the boat; others simply prefer to go out and warm up in the canoe. Either way, it is important to paddle for at least ten minutes before any race. Paddle slowly at first, with a relaxed motion focusing on technique and on stretching out your specific paddling muscles. Once you feel loose, put in one or two short but hard efforts at about 80-90% maximum and then paddle slowly again. At this point, some racers like to get out of the boat and relax before the start while others prefer to stay in the canoe until the start itself. Either way, you will be physically and mentally prepared.

Photograph by Dick Mansfield

Double-check all your equipment before the race.

Comprehensive Race Plan

Before you and your partner paddle out toward the starting line, you should discuss and agree upon an overall race plan. While things almost never go strictly according to plan, it is important to develop a strategy for the race. This overall plan should take into account your strengths and weaknesses, the level of competition, the race course, the time of year, and your race objectives. What do you really want out of this race?

Let's look at a few issues you should talk over before getting into the boat. What are you using this race for? Is it a "training race" to help sharpen pack-riding skills? Are you trying to build speed and peak for the Nationals? Are you going all-out for a win in your class? Is the course predominantly shallow or deep? Do you plan to run with a first or second pack until the upstream section and then go for it? Do you plan on attacking at every opportunity, or are you hoping to lay back and grind teams down that cannot keep up the pace? Do you just want to work on endurance and finish strong?

Having a comprehensive "game plan" will not only assure that both partners have the same expectations, it also will help both of you communicate and react appropriately to situations during the race. Finally, you will be able to evaluate each race with a view towards what you were and were not able to accomplish. This facilitates planning for future training and racing.

At The Starting Line

There is no more important part of a canoe race than the start. While you will not win the race at the start, you may lose it here. You can be guaranteed of this: at the start of any race it's going to be fast and it's going to be wild.

Most canoe racers will want to be in front or at least with the front pack at the start because otherwise, it is a major disadvantage to have to cope with the wakes and irregular waves of the leading canoes. The closer you are to the front after the start, the fewer energy-sapping irregular wakes you will have to deal with. Good racers go hard off the line, so if you want to be competitive, you're going to have to go hard as well. I've never known a canoe race to have been won by someone who takes it easy off the starting line.

If, on the other hand, you are new to canoe racing or are unsure of your boat handling skills, it may make a lot of sense to take it easy and let the fast canoes get out of your way. Then you can sort yourself out and hopefully start passing some canoes. As you gain skill, it will be absolutely essential to develop the fastest possible start.

The first thing to consider as the start of a race approaches is the nature of the starting line itself. Is it wide? Is it narrow? Is one portion of the line deeper than others? Is there a place in the line where there is more current? Most race organizers try to have their race start where there is no significant advantage at any portion of the starting line over another, but if there are advantageous places to be on the line, you want to be there.

Next, you need to decide where you want to start in relation to the competition. If you feel that you will be one of the fastest canoes on the line, you will probably want to line up next to some of the more experienced teams, in the hope that you will not be bumped and can get away cleanly. Likewise, if you feel confident in your ability to ride wake, you may want to line up next to one of the better teams, hoping they will pull you away from the mass of confusion right after the start. If you lack confidence in your boat handling skills but still want to get as fast a start as possible, it's smart to move to either end of the starting line, where the likelihood of interference is least. Some fast teams, at a mass start, will line up beside a recreational boat or slow team. This gives them a clean start, after which they begin to position themselves towards the best teams for wake riding.

The starting line of some races, particularly major races, can become crowded — you end up packed in gunnel to gunnel. One way to give yourself more room is to originally line up a little crooked. Shortly before the gun goes off, straighten the canoe out. This should give both you and your partner some room to paddle. If the boats next to you close in tightly and there is no time to move to a different position on the line, then just do your best to at least get your blade down in the water for the start. Sometimes it's possible to get the paddlers next to you to agree to paddle on the same side of their respective canoes so you don't interfere with each other for at least the first few strokes. In the worst case scenario, the bow person will almost always be able to paddle but the stern person may have to rudder for a few strokes until room develops.

The Start

It's important to develop your own starting technique and strategy. The goal is to accelerate your canoe from a standing start to maximum hull speed as quickly as possible. Each racer comes at this problem differently based on their physiological makeup and their own preferred technique. Some paddlers, like Montana's Mike Johnson, come off the line with huge powerful strokes, keeping the stroke rate relatively slow. Others, such as Nick Bauer from the State of Washington, accelerate the canoe with a series of quick, yet powerful strokes at a high stroke rate. In a C-2, many teams practice going as many as 12 to 18 strokes on one side before calling the first "hut" to switch sides. This can give you an edge on the teams that quickly switch 2 or 3 times right off the line.

Because starting is so important, it is something that must be practiced. After a good deal of personal experimentation and practice, you will discover what technique works best for you. A polished and practiced starting technique will help ensure that you get off the line fast every time.

Courtesy Le nouvelliste

At the start, both paddlers must have arms extended,
ready for the first stroke when the gun sounds.

Starting line procedure varies from race to race, but you will usually be given an oral warning before the starting gun goes off. The key is to be prepared; don't let the gun go off with you waving to your friends on shore. In the C-2 boat, both paddlers must be in agreement on the procedure they're going to use at the gun, and the stern person will have to concentrate particularly hard to match strokes with the bow person in the chaos of the start.

Courtesy Le Nouvelliste

A rope start at the Classique Internationale de Canots. Note how stern padders must position themselves to hold the rope.

Most races today use buoys to indicate the starting line. At a buoy start, keep the bow of your boat on the buoy line. Both paddlers should have arms extended, ready for that all-important catch and power phase of the first stroke. Try to keep your canoe still just before the gun or even allow a slight drift forward. Under no circumstances do you want to be caught backpaddling or drifting backwards when the gun goes off.

Some of the major races utilize a rope start. In such a start, a rope is stretched across the river and pulled as tightly as possible, normally suspended above the river level by a foot or two. On a rope start, you need to get <u>downstream</u> of the start and then back into the position you want on the line. Do not try to approach the rope from upriver because this forces you to lift the rope or duck under it to get into position. Even in top pro races, where people are supposed to know better, there will inevitably be one or two teams trying to approach the rope from above. The result is usually a quick flip and a cold swim — not the ideal way to begin your race.

Once you have backed into position, the stern person should grab the rope with one hand, holding the lower shaft of the paddle with the other. The bow paddler will be at the ready. On the gun, the stern paddler lets go of the rope, grabs the top handle of the paddle, and gets in synch with the bow paddler during the first stroke.

Getting Away From The Line

The heaviest traffic and most confusion you are likely to encounter in any race will occur during the first several hundred yards immediately after the start. Everyone is fresh. Everyone will be sprinting like mad. Some people will be going straight. Some people will not. With all the boats sprinting, the waves will be huge. You can be assured of one thing: it's going to be exciting.

At this earliest stage in the race, you have two primary goals: First, to get away from the line as fast as you can and establish the best possible position; and second, to avoid getting trashed by other canoes that may be out of control. As soon as you have your canoe up to maximum hull speed, concentrate on settling into good, crisp technique and focus on maintaining a straight line. The best way to do this during the first 20 or 30 yards away from the starting line is to focus on a object in the distance, such as a tree or point of land, and use it as a directional target. It won't be long, however, before you will have to abandon the straight line of your "game plan" and adjust to what is happening on either side of you.

The most important thing to remember during those early chaotic moments is to work on being aware of everything going on around you. The first "deadly sin" committed by most beginning and novice canoe racers is that they will simply put their heads down and bull their canoe straight ahead — no matter what. It goes

Photograph by Jim Adams

Canoe race starts, like the start of the 1991 Michigan Marathon
on the Ausable River, are exciting for paddlers and spectators.

without fail that after the start of nearly every canoe race, one or
more such teams will either be running into other racers, or being
smashed themselves, and they will alter their line or their technique
not a wit. This "bull in a china shop" strategy is ineffective, and it
won't be long before these teams are out of contention. The sad part
is that they may take other teams with them.

> In order to get away from the starting line fast and ef-
> fectively, you've got to be aware of who is doing
> what, and you have to react accordingly. In a C-2, it
> is particularly important for the stern person to keep
> an overall view as to what's happening. The stern
> person's perspective is much better than that of the
> person in the bow. He or she will know whether or
> not another team is veering into the canoe and will
> be able to adjust accordingly. So keep your head up
> and practice using your peripheral vision to get the
> big picture. Tunnel vision usually results in being
> left back in the tunnel.

The only team that has the luxury of choosing their course without great concern for the position of other competitors is the team in the lead. If you are fast enough and perhaps lucky enough to find yourself in the lead, your tactical options are simplified. If you have been able to quickly drop teams off your wake and it appears you may be able to dominate the race, then go for it. If you can open up that gap and nobody can go with you, then it will be to your advantage to break contact with your competition early on and create a larger and larger lead. In this situation it is best to go hard, but stay aerobic. You're obviously only going to be able to maintain your all-out sprint for a short while and you'll want to settle into your fastest possible aerobic race pace. The competition will have to be doing the same thing and, as long as you are able to maintain your lead or increase it, your best strategy is to grind it out. Unless you totally bonk, it will be rare that your competition will be able to catch you. Often the other teams will start looking at each other and forget about trying to reel you in.

Courtesy Le Nouvelliste

Waves are huge and collisions frequent just after the start.

Teams that have gotten into the early lead but are not able to shake one or more competitors off their wake will have to consider other alternatives. If the lead team just continues to grind away, the competition will simply sit on the wake and ride, waiting for the leaders to burn out. If you find yourself in such a lead position, consider backing off and allowing one or more teams to come up on your side wakes, particularly if these are teams you can work with. Let them share in taking the lead and pulling, while you ride. This type of strategy will be particularly helpful if you are a team that has a high sprint speed but which is not particularly adept at grinding it out over long stretches of the river. You will want to ride "the grinders" and then try to outsprint them in shallow water or at the finish.

If you are not fast enough or lucky enough to sprint to the lead, you'll have to deal with other boats, waves, and general chaos until things settle down. Try to find a canoe near you which is going approximately the same speed (or ideally a little faster), and jump on the stern wake or the side wake and go with them. Don't be intimidated by the size of the waves created by the mass of sprinting canoes. Think of them as an opportunity — a "gift" of energy. It will be "surf's up" time, so if you feel one of these large starting area waves picking your canoe up at the stern, both paddlers should sprint the canoe to top speed and try to get on. Once you're on the wave, you can relax your intensity and ride it forward.

If you find the bow of your canoe plowing into a large wave, you should either back off your pace and pick up the wave behind, or you should sprint over the wave in front and ride it. Whatever you do, don't waste energy by plowing ahead with your bow up on a big wave. Sprint over it and ride, or drop back and take the next one.

If any canoe catches you from behind and begins to go by, try not to let it go without making a serious attempt to ride its wake, either from the side or behind. Chances are that these racers may be good grinders with a high cruise speed, or they may simply have gotten badly bumped at the start and are recovering. Either way, they may be your ticket to the front.

If your canoe becomes the unwitting victim of a bad collision with a canoe which is out of control, there are a number of ways to prevent disaster. First, the bow person should attempt to keep paddling under almost all circumstances — the only reason the bow person should stop is to brace to prevent a flip. Second, the stern paddler must react according to the situation. Because the stern paddler can see and diagnose what is going on, it will be up to him or her to take the necessary action to limit the potential damage.

If your canoe is getting hit in the bow area, the stern person should hut the bow paddler to the side opposite the one being hit and both paddlers should continue to paddle forward. If your canoe is being struck in the rear portion (the old "T-Bone" as it's known), it is highly likely that you may be driven radically off to the left or the right. In this dangerous circumstance the stern person must immediately hut so that he or she is paddling on the opposite side from the colliding canoe and then, with the paddle, hold a hard rudder, literally pushing the stern of your canoe back in towards the offending canoe. The leverage advantage is with the stern person throwing the rudder. So long as your bow person keeps paddling, you will not only be able to hold your line, but you may be able to send the offending canoe off out of harm's way.

If either through inexperience or because you got hit and shoved into another canoe, you end up being the offender instead of the victim in this scenario, your best strategy usually will be to back off and allow the canoe you have hit to clear. It is not simply a matter of being polite — if you keep plowing forward, you will continue to run into the other canoe and neither boat will go anywhere fast. Also, the racers in the canoe you have hit will be none too pleased if you continue to drive them into the bushes or another canoe. This is definitely not the way to make friends and influence people on the racing circuit.

If you're not right up with the leaders shortly after the start, do not panic, there's plenty of race left. Under normal circumstances, and especially in deep water, the leaders will slow down after they have established themselves in the front. This is often because the top boats are "feeling each other out" in terms of determining who has the best sprint speed and who is going well on that particular day. It is also a recognition of the fact that the race is a long one, so the top teams are not going to use up their energy in the early going.

It's in this early stage, during the first five to fifteen minutes of a race, that you should have a good opportunity to bridge up to the pack. Try to move up with a series of sprints and recoveries. Sprint close enough to ride one of the back wakes of a lead boat for a few moments, recover, then attempt to attack forward to the next wave. Once you gain that wave, rest again. It is often helpful to keep your "huts" as soft as possible while doing this, so as not to attract undue attention to the fact that you are coming up on the leaders.

If you have any likelihood of getting up with the leader or the lead pack of any canoe race, you almost always have to do it in the early going. Once that front group pulls away to a significant lead and breaks contact with you, the likelihood of having a chance to win the race is tiny indeed. You may be able to pick off refugees from the front pack as they tire and drop away, but it is difficult to regain the leaders. So, if you are going to make a move to the front, both paddlers have to resolve to dig down and do it early in the race. Whether you accomplish this through a long all-out grind or with a series of sprints and recoveries, the effort will take something out of you, but the rewards are usually worth it.

After clearing the starting line and evaluating the situation, if it becomes clear that you are not going to catch the leaders or the front pack, then you must decide what strategy will result in the best possible placing at the end of the race. If you are a good grinding team with a decent cruise speed, you may wish to race along alone. On the other hand, if you have more of a sprint and recovery style, you may want to slow down a bit and attempt to work with other boats to form a second or third pack.

The Unwritten Rules Of The Pack

In marathon canoe racing there are few moments as exciting as running with a pack of canoes. The group dynamics are complex and intriguing. Every action of one team affects all of the other teams. With canoes each taking a turn sprinting or "pulling," while the other canoes rest on the side or back waves, the pack can move forward at a faster consistent pace than any one canoe alone. On the other hand, if it is not to the advantage for any of the canoes to be "pulling," the pack as a whole may slow down. Either way, the canoe racers within that pack, as they ride each other's wakes, are expending much less energy than their competitors who are out on the river alone.

Photograph by Inner Mountain

Top mixed teams form a five boat front pack at the 1988 USCA Nationals and ride each other's wakes to conserve energy.

When you find yourself riding with a fairly large pack, particularly in the early stages of a race, the racing can seem so easy that you may not feel you are working as hard as you should. Don't fight it. Enjoy it while it lasts, because you're actually moving along fast and expending little energy doing it. You will know what I mean the very first time you get dropped after riding for a while with a pack.

I first learned of the energy saved in a pack during my initial try at racing the famous International Classic in Quebec. For the first day's leg, which is approximately eight hours long, my partner and I managed to come together with four other canoes and form a nice second pack. Neither of us were very experienced at this sort of thing and it simply felt too easy. We kept looking behind us, expecting to be overtaken, but the canoes to our immediate rear were not getting any closer. My partner and I kept talking about "hitting it" and bringing the pace up for a while but we felt too inexperienced to make any decisive moves.

Suddenly we hit shallow water; the pack sprinted; and we fell two waves back. Now we had to sprint with everything we had, and we still didn't seem to be able to regain the pack. We struggled in the irregular waves thrown off the back of the pack, zigging and zagging and finally, after about ten minutes of maximum effort, were able to regain the side wake of the pack. Ahhh! It suddenly felt so easy again. That ten minute maximum effort had nearly exhausted us, but the lesson was driven home. The pack as a whole was moving fast, even though the energy expenditure of the individual pack members was far lower than would be required of a single team trying to keep the same pace. When I finally regained my breath and could talk, I asked my bow partner if he was content to sit where we were and he quickly shook his head yes. I couldn't have agreed more.

Photograph by Dick Mansfield

The energy spent by each team in a pack is far less than that of a single team trying to keep pace.

When the water's deep and the race is in its early stages, the pack can slow down to such an extent that it feels darn near like relaxation. In these circumstances, the racers often let down their competitive fronts and chit chat with each other. During a long race, pack members will often take this opportunity to eat and drink. Even jokes get told.

You won't find any rule books where it tells you what to do when you get in a pack, but there are certain unwritten rules which all savvy canoe racers understand and which are usually obeyed. The penalty for violating these rules depends upon the severity of the indiscretion — either you will be shunned by the pack (that is everyone will avoid paddling near you), or everyone will simply try to drop you off the back.

Here are some of the most important of the unwritten rules of the pack:

Keep your canoe going straight and avoid hitting other canoes. There is nothing more aggravating than a canoe zigzagging and out of control. An occasional minor bump is bound to happen, but if you are continuously bashing into other canoes, the pack will make sure you are not around long.

The lead canoe has the right of way and sets the line. Everyone in the pack must react to the direction in which the lead canoe team chooses to go. That is, if the lead canoe team chooses to turn to the left, then the canoes riding wake in the pack must also adjust and turn left. If you don't like the direction the lead canoe team is going, pull up and take the lead — then you can set the course.

Take your turn at the front. As long as you are not sick or "bonked" and just hanging on, it is considered good form to share the pulling chores. The pull is not a sprint; it is a strong and steady effort which will allow the other canoes in the pack to ride your wave. And a pull does not have to be particularly long — 30 seconds to a minute at the front will suffice.

When you're in close quarters, adjust your stroke technique so that you are not striking the canoe or the paddles of the boat next to you. This can usually be accomplished by keeping the recovery phase of your stroke close to your own canoe. The stern person can also time the "huts" to minimize conflict with adjoining paddlers.

Never, ever touch another person's canoe with your hand!

Warn another paddler if the bow of your canoe is in a position where he or she may strike it with his or her paddle. Hitting somebody's bow with the flat face of a carbon racing paddle is the quickest way I know to force you to go to your spare.

If you are getting sucked into the side of another team's canoe which is ahead of you, it is your responsibility to draw or pry away to avoid a collision. This is especially so if your bow is getting sucked into the stern area of an opponent's canoe. A hard hit in this area can drive the other canoe sideways or even flip it over. You may gain a momentary advantage in this one particular race but you will not be welcome back in the pack.

If you are moving up from the stern wake to the side wake and coming between two canoes, be sure not to make your move unless there is sufficient room for you. It gets awfully aggravating when people try to force three canoes into a two canoe-wide space. At the same time, it is generally not considered to be good form to intentionally bring your boat closer to another simply to squeeze out a canoe between you.

Don't intentionally splash paddlers or put water into the canoe of competitors who are properly riding your side wake. The technique of splashing water into the canoe of a competitor is only utilized by a stern person when there is a canoe team hanging on your back wave and you want to get rid of them.

Don't attack or sprint when a team is eating. In long races, all the canoe teams in a pack are going to have to periodically eat. It's bad manners to attack when teams are eating. This is one of those rules of common sense and politeness which, while getting violated on occasion, makes a great deal of sense. You will certainly have to eat too — you don't want the other teams attacking when you have a handful of fruit.

Rest, relax, and enjoy when you are in a pack of canoes. The whole purpose of being in the pack in the first place is to allow you to cruise along at a high rate of speed while utilizing significantly less energy stores. Your ride in the pack will be the perfect time to eat, drink, and to try to work out stiffness in those sore neck and shoulder muscles. So rest and enjoy your time in the pack; if you're there, you've earned it.

Attacking Strategies

Let's assume that you are now well into the race but still feel strong and fast. You and your partner have plenty in reserve and it appears as if the teams around you may be tiring. What are some of the best strategies and techniques to use to catch teams ahead of you and drop teams that may be with you?

Catching A Canoe

There are several basic approaches when attempting to catch a team that is out in front of you. If you are not yet close enough to that team to begin to feel the effects of any of their wake, then your best strategy is either to grind closer to the team in front with a long sustained effort or, utilize a series of one to two minute interval surges at near-maximum effort punctuated by "easier" one to two minute rest periods where you try to cruise at a speed at least no slower than the team you are attempting to overtake. If you are moving generally faster than the team in front of you, either method will bring you to a point where you will begin to be able to take advantage of your competitor's wake.

In deep water you are now faced with essentially two basic alternative tactics. The first is to go either wide right or left, moving completely outside the inverted "V" wake of the lead boat. In this smooth water you can now employ either the grinding strategy or the interval strategy discussed above. If, on the other hand, you decide to stay within the inverted "V" wake, then you need to employ a strategy which will utilize the various waves you will encounter as you close in on the lead boat. In deep water this normally means three or four significant lines of stern waves that will have to be surmounted before finally getting into a position just behind the lead boat. The best way to accomplish this is to angle slightly to the left or the right(still within the inverted "V" wake area) and sprint over the waves out where they are lower. Once you have jumped your canoe up and over the wave, you can slide back into a position directly behind the lead boat and ride the wave until you recover sufficiently to attack again.

Then repeat the process — jumping the wave and riding — until you find yourself on the first wave right behind the lead canoe. From there you are in position to attack up to the side wake of the lead canoe, either left or right side as dictated by the situation.

Photograph by Dick Mansfield

The trailing boat is well-positioned to jump from the second stern wave to the first stern wave and then up on a side wake.

When the water is shallow, it is very difficult to utilize effectively the stern waves being thrown off by the lead canoe. In such low water conditions, it is usually better to get out over the side wake of the lead boat and advance in the calm water which is unaffected by the lead boat's wake.

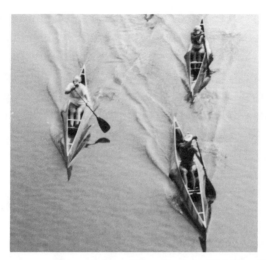

Photograph by Dick Mansfield

Women C-1 paddlers repetitively attack to try to drop the competition.

Dropping A Canoe

There are many techniques and strategies for dropping a canoe or canoes that are hanging with you. There is no one right or wrong way to do this, but there are certain basic moves which you can adapt to a wide variety of competitive conditions.

Whenever you are approaching shallow water, you should be prepared to attack. Shallow water of any type presents the best opportunity to drop other canoes. Whether you have canoes on your side wake or stern wake, it will be very difficult for them to stay there if you are the first boat sprinting into the shallow water.

A short stretch of shallow water, such as you find on the inside of a turn, can be effective for dropping a canoe one or two waves back. The key here is to accelerate your boat to sprint speed so that you get into the shallow water first. As we have seen in previous chapters, the waves will build in size and shorten in wave length, making them very difficult to ride. The end result is that you may be able to shed the canoe or canoes that have been dogging you and quickly open up a lead of several canoe lengths. Once you have them off your side wave or first back wave, it's time to put the hammer down and not let them come back.

Every C-2 team needs to be able to initiate an attack without broadcasting the upcoming move to the world. Yelling to the bow paddler, "Let's Sprint!" is not likely to catch anyone by surprise.

Either member of a C-2 team must be able to signal a sprint, based upon what he or she observes, and communicate that fact to the partner without letting the competitors know. Bow persons often initiate sprints, particularly on mixed teams where the substantially heavier and more powerful "sprint machine" is usually in the bow. When this happens, no verbal communication is needed. The stern person should always be aware of precisely what is going on in the bow and be able to react to any changes of intensity that the bow person initiates. When the bow person goes hard, the stern paddler simply must be ready to react at once and go with the same intensity.

If a stern person is signalling the sprint, it usually calls for some sort of verbal signal. Some teams do this by calling the "hut" in a different tone, or by using another word in place of "hut." Partners who have paddled together for a period of time find that no verbal signal is necessary. Experienced bow paddlers can often just feel the dramatic change in their partner's stroke and respond accordingly.

Coming into a portage is always a good time for an attack. If you can get into the portage first, the likelihood is that gaps will open. Once you put back in the water after the portage and have some distance on the canoes behind, it's again time to work hard and try to increase your lead, or at least make your competitors expend a great deal of energy trying to catch you.

Deep water situations require the competitor to be a bit more creative in order to pull off a successful attack. The problem here is that the deep water waves are going to be easy for your competitors to ride and it will be much simpler for them to cover any attack you might make. You need to develop the ability to quickly change your boat speed from a fast cruise to an all-out sprint, without broadcasting what you are about to do to your competitors.

Quick acceleration is the first ingredient to any successful attack, and the only way you develop it is to practice "jumps" in your training sessions. It is absolutely imperative to be able to accelerate your canoe from a high cruise speed to all-out sprint speed within two or three strokes. You want to catch your competitors unaware, and you want to get enough of a jump on them before they can react and cover.

When trying to pull off a successful sprint on a canoe or group of canoes waking you, it is often helpful to throw in a change of direction at the same time. For instance, if you have a canoe on your right side wake and you suddenly take a sharp turn to the left and sprint, the turn maneuver alone will drop the competitor's canoe back half a boat length. This may be all you need to break contact. One of the favored methods for setting up this turn change is to first gradually bear in toward the canoe with you, causing those paddlers to react by pulling away, to prevent boat contact. While they are busy reacting in this fashion, you suddenly turn, go the other way, and sprint. This is a most difficult tactic to defend against and should be part of every team's attacking repertoire.

An effective attacking method is to do a series of sprints and rests, so that you get your competition into a rhythm. Just as soon as they have figured out that you are going to be sprinting for 30 seconds and resting for 30 seconds, you might try sprinting for over a minute in the hopes that your competition will automatically and subconsciously begin to ease off after 30 seconds. Another technique is to sprint for 30 seconds and begin to ease off for just a few seconds and then suddenly attack again.

If you're feeling particularly strong, you can attack other waking canoes again and again and again, in the hopes of wearing down the weaker teams. This technique can be effective, but it also has its dangers. If a team is able to cover the attacks and ride easily while you are sprinting, this strong team may simply wait till your energy is beginning to wane and then suddenly attack on its own.

This happened at the 1991 National Championships in Marinette, Wisconsin. In the early stages of the race, Bob Zaveral and Bob MacDowell were extremely strong, attacking again and again off the front of the pack. While many racers were having difficulties staying with these numerous attacks, the team of Bruce Barton and Calvin Hassel were not. They were able to ride out each attack fairly comfortably and as soon as the water began to shallow, launched their own attack, catching Zaveral and MacDowell drained. As a result, Barton and Hassel, along with a few other canoes got away.

The repetitive attack technique can be very effective, but you must be careful that you are not working so hard that you are, in effect, acting as a "rabbit" for some of the other teams. The danger here obviously most often occurs in deep water. But repeated attacks by a strong team in shallow water are often very difficult to defend against. Only the fastest and most skilled teams will be able to hang on.

What usually happens in a pack is that a rhythm is established whereby one team will sprint and all the other teams will accelerate to ride that team's wake, until the sprinting team gradually slows down, usually after 20 seconds to a minute or two. Everyone will then ride along easily for a period of time until another team feels in an advantageous position and attacks. Another attacking technique which is seldom used but particularly effective is to immediately launch an attack right after a team which has just sprinted is backing off on its pace. If you feel strong enough to attack as soon as a previously attacking team slows down, you can often catch many teams off their guard and tired.

You do not necessarily need to be the lead boat to attack. One of the most effective ways in which to drop another canoe is to attack off a side wake. This is executed by riding another canoe's side wake as comfortably as possible, waiting for this canoe to turn slightly away from you. (All racing canoes tend to zig-zag slightly down the course and you simply want to catch the lead boat while it is zigging slightly away from you.) Instead of adjusting your canoe to stay parallel, as you would do if you were trying to sit on the side wake, you angle off in the other direction, accelerating and getting a little boost from the side wake. In this manner, you can often get away before the lead boat has time to react. If you can't get rid of the competition, you will at least make them work very hard and expend a great deal of energy trying to cover your moves.

Photograph by Dick Mansfield

A good time to attack off the side wake is when the lead boat veers slightly away from you.

It is also possible to attack from a stern wake position. One of the most commonly used ways to carry this off involves the "sling-shot" technique. In this situation, you would set up your canoe by riding the first stern wave, either to the left side or right side of the lead canoe. To initiate the attack, you begin to slide your canoe across the stern wave, going behind the lead canoe, and angling out to the opposite side. You should be in a full sprint by the time you hit and jump the angled side wave, getting a sling-shot boost from a combination of the rear wake and angled side wake. When you put the hammer down and go for it, this can be a difficult attacking strategy to cover. If nothing else, it will surely get you up onto the side wake of the lead canoe.

Defending Strategies

Okay, now things are not going so well. You're getting tired; it's becoming harder and harder to stay with the other canoes when they sprint. Whether you've run out of food or water, or whether you've simply paddled to the limits that your training time will take you, you know that your speed is gone. Randy Drake has an apt name for it: he calls it "Backwards Time." When you are at your limits, when it's time to go backwards, what is the best way to limit your loss?

First, you have to determine how bad off you really are. If you have come to the absolute end of your glycogen stores and simply have nothing left, there is only so much you will be able to do. Some athletes call this "the bonk" or "hitting the wall" or being "trashed" — but when it happens to you, you know what it is. Your energy gas tank is on empty.

Feeling this bad, you're probably not going to be able to ride anybody's wave or cover any attacks, yet there's no need to simply give up or drop out of the race. You can continue racing at a decent pace if you concentrate on maintaining good technique and keeping your stroke rate up. You will be surprised to see how far good technique will carry you, even when the power is gone. You may want to shorten the power phase of your stroke slightly and will obviously have a lesser amount of "power" in this phase, but don't let the rest of your technique change. It is still critically important to maintain the speed of your recovery phase and to continually get a good catch. Forget speedwork of any kind — that's done for the day. However, if another canoe catches you but is not going a great deal faster, try to ride a back wave and rest as much as possible. Perhaps you'll be lucky enough to get "towed" to the finish line.

If you are getting tired but have not completely bonked, you will want to settle into a steady pace which you can maintain and eat and drink as you try to replenish your energy stores. If you have really hit the wall, eating and drinking will not bring you back, but if you are in the early stages of running out of glycogen, a well-timed banana or energy bar will do wonders.

Once you start going backwards, you are going to need a little help from your friends. In this case, your friends are every canoe that catches you. Each one of these canoes is trailing a number of side waves and back waves and each one of those waves is like a gift of energy to you. Do not let those gifts of energy go by without attempting to utilize them.

If you are in shallow water, or if the overtaking canoe is going at a speed much greater than yours, it will be difficult to ride any of the waves for a significant length of time. But don't let this deter you. Try for any wave that may give you even the slightest break.

Photograph by Dick Mansfield

Two trailing men's teams at the 1990 Nationals sprint to cover the sudden attack by the lead canoe.

When you are lucky enough to be caught by a steadily overtaking canoe in deep water, you may have just found your ticket to the finish line. As the canoe is coming on you, slide your canoe over so that you are within 5 to 15 feet of the overtaking canoe. First, try to ride on the side wake by increasing the pace as the wave picks up your stern. If this is too energy consuming, don't hesitate to fall back to the first stern wave. Try to bring your canoe up to a speed whereby you can ride a wave, even if it means expending some of your vital reserve energy. The reward of energy savings will be worth it. If you can't hang onto that first wave, then let your canoe go back until the stern is picked up by the second wave. Perhaps you can ride this wave, or even the third wave.

If you simply cannot stay with that canoe, don't struggle. Let go and continue to paddle along steadily, waiting for the next canoe to get you. Each successive canoe which catches you is likely to be going slower than the last one. This means that with each canoe, you will have a better chance to get a good ride and a much needed rest. By doing this, you may be able to prevent yourself from going backwards any farther.

In most cases, you will be able to finish a race and finish it effectively, even though you have run out of gas. You may not be able to sprint over any more waves or cover any more attacks, but you will usually be able to grind it to the finish line. But, if you are in really bad shape and consider yourself to be in any sort of medical jeopardy, do not hesitate to pull yourself out of the race. No race is so important that you should jeopardize your health. There will always be another race and another river to paddle.

Buoy Turns

Buoy turns are almost always tactically significant. If you are with other canoes as you approach a buoy turn, you can be assured that the pace will increase and each canoe around you will jockey for optimum position coming into and out of the turn. If you happen to be alone when you hit a buoy turn, you simply want to be sure to execute the turn as efficiently as possible. (See Chapter 4 for proper buoy turn technique.)

If you can, you want to be the first boat into the buoy turn. The sharp deceleration and turn can open up gaps quickly. There's a great opportunity for one or more lead canoes in the pack to drop the rest of the pack back one or two waves after the buoy.

If you manage to come to the buoy turn first, keep your turn as tight as possible. Don't worry about canoes that are outside you. They will be having enough trouble staying parallel to your boat and fighting being shot off by your side wake. The real threat may likely come from a canoe coming up behind you on the inside. For example, if you are making a sharp clockwise turn to the right, expect the canoe behind to come up fast on the inside, your right. There's a good chance that the following canoe will hit your boat in the stern area so your stern paddler must be ready to throw in a quick rudder stroke on the left side of the canoe to prevent being pushed completely sideways. Once the situation has stabilized, it's often best for the lead canoe to go to "sides" so that both racers are paddling on the left side. This accomplishes two things: it holds the canoe on a hard line while at the same time providing excellent acceleration as you exit the turn.

If you happen to be second, third, or further back in a line of canoes heading into a buoy turn, then do your best to keep your bow to the inside of the stern of the boat in front of you. By riding the inside of the stern wave, it will be easier to hold a tight line and to come out of the turn quickly. If you happen to come up and nudge the boat in front of you, it will actually help hold you on the inside line. If you are well-positioned, and if the boat in front executes the turn poorly and swings wide, you will have the opportunity to jump up on the inside wake, and perhaps even make a break.

If you can't take an inside line to the buoy and find yourself caught on the outside of several canoes heading into a buoy turn, there are several ways to prevent a disastrous wide turn. First, always try to keep your canoe parallel to and as close as possible to the canoe on the inside. Get right up there; don't allow your bow to drift back any farther than the position of the bow paddler of the inside canoe. It will be easier to ride the side wake in this forward position. If you let your boat slip farther back, it becomes more likely that the side wake will throw you off into a wide turn. Second, try to maintain a constant distance of a few feet between your team and the inside canoe. Third, as you come out of the turn, both bow and stern paddler should paddle on the off-side — that is, the side farthest away from the canoe taking the inside line. This will help hold you parallel to the inside canoe while at the same time providing excellent acceleration as you emerge from the turn.

If you have a bad buoy turn, either by swinging too wide or by taking several bad bumps, recover as quickly as possible. Regroup and close down any gap that has opened up between you and the boats that you were with. The longer you allow a gap to exist in such a situation, the more difficult it will be to jump the gap. Attack right after the turn; jump the waves you need to; get back with the pack.

Using Pit Teams

The unsung heroes of any successful long-distance canoe team are known as "pit teams," "support teams," or "bank runners." These are the people who tirelessly follow the paddlers down the river, supplying them with fresh drink jugs, food, spare paddles, clothing, or whatever else is needed for the team to keep going. It is not a glamorous job, but no team racing long distances could be successful without such support. In any race longer than two to three hours duration, you must consider the necessity of a support crew. The most commonly needed items are new jugs with cold liquid and energy-supplying food. If you are going to go fast and if you are going to go long, then you must be well-versed in the proper use of a pit team.

While it is possible for one person to act as a support crew for a C-2 racing team, this is not recommended unless the support person is extremely experienced. You should have two people to act as support, one assigned to helping the bow person and the other charged with the support of the stern person.

Pit Crew Technique In Shallow Water

If a river is fairly narrow and shallow, and the weather is not cold, the pit team will probably be able to wade into the water and be in a position that will not take the canoe team far off its line. Narrow, shallow, and twisting rivers such as the General Clinton's Susquehanna and Michigan's Ausable are ideal for this method of pit positioning. If your crew cannot wade far enough into the

Photograph by Dick Mansfield

Shallow water provides an excellent pit stop.

current and be positioned so that the canoe crew can be pitted
without a major alteration of their course, an alternate feeding
method should be considered.

> Plan out the pit situations carefully before the race
> and write down a plan. Don't hesitate to talk to more
> experienced racers — paddlers who know the river
> well. Estimate your arrival times and make sure your
> crew knows what you want replenished. Then, your
> crew will know when to expect you at different pit
> spots along the route and be there and ready with
> the proper food and drink when you show up. The
> schedule can easily be adjusted once the race is
> underway — you'll often hear racers say to their
> crew, "I'm running ten minutes behind," or "How
> about a Power Bar at the next pit?"

Your pit team should wade into the water in anticipation of the arrival of their paddlers and stand so that they do not interfere with other canoe teams that pass by. They should be situated so that their paddlers do not have to go out of the way to get pitted. As the paddlers approach the feed zone, they will normally jettison their empty jugs. The pit team then places the new jugs and food in the canoe as the paddlers go by. The paddlers will adjust the containers into place. If done properly, the racers need not slow down significantly and little time is lost. The pit crews then will have plenty of time to retrieve the used containers and get ready to head out to the next stop. Pit crews are often well-tanned and well-read!

Photograph by Tricia Heed

Smooth pit team work means little loss of time during fuel stops.

Some support crews prefer to place the jugs directly in the jug holders and the food in the food containers as the canoe passes by. However, this is often easier said than done, especially in a closely bunched pack of canoes. A common method is to simply drop the jug and food bags on the floor of the canoe between the paddler's legs. Then, when it is convenient (such as when they have regained the wake of the canoe in front of them), the racers can place the jugs, straighten out the drink tube, and put the food in the food container.

Pits During A Portage

One of the best opportunities to resupply a canoe team is at any portage. Since all the canoes must get out of the water anyway, the portage provides easy access and a perfect situation to exchange drink jugs and replace food. The accepted method is for the canoe team to jettison the empty jugs at the approach to the portage or at the very beginning of the portage. The team can then run the portage with the canoe being as light as possible. The support team should be waiting at the put-in, where either of two feeding methods can be utilized. Some teams prefer to receive their feed just before going into the water. If this method is used, the canoe racers will need to lower the boat about waist high and in a right-side-up position. The support people quickly place the jugs and food in the proper containers and then the canoe team runs down to the water. Alternately, if the put-in is relatively shallow, the feeders can be waiting in the water. Here, after the racers put the boat in the water and while they are clambering into their seats, the pit crew quickly places the jugs and food.

It's important to remember that you should not sit there after a portage and attempt to adjust your feeder tubes or your food. This loses critical time. Instead, get underway immediately and adjust the drinking system and food after you are out in the current or securely riding someone's wake.

Pitting From A Canoe

When the river is too wide and deep to pit from the shore or shallows and if there are no convenient portages, your best solution is to pit from another boat. This method is used almost exclusively during the first day of the International Classique in Quebec where the St. Maurice River is wide, deep, and there are no portages for the full 70-plus mile length.

Pitting from another canoe can be very effective, but it requires a pit crew who know how to handle a canoe and who will not be intimidated by a pack of canoes bearing down on them. As on shore, it is possible for a highly experienced solo person to pit a team from a C-1, but it is much better, where possible, to utilize two people in a C-2. The chances of mistakes or problems occurring when you have two people are much less. When pitting from a canoe, the pit team must locate themselves right in the main current in such a way that their racing team will not have to change course in order to get support. This is particularly important where the racing team is drafting with one or more other canoes. There is nothing more frustrating for canoe racers than to work hard to get on the wake of another canoe, only to have to abandon that wake because the pit crew is way out of position.

Some boat pit crews line up so that they are paddling in the direction of their race team. As their team approaches, the pit crew begins to paddle slowly forward and they execute the exchange as the racing team goes by. If done properly, the race team need only slow down slightly to effectuate the transfer. While it is the responsibility of the pit boat to be lined up as close as possible to the course of the racing team, it is the job of the racers to be sure that they paddle close enough to their pit boat and slow down enough to allow the exchange. When handling the boat pit in this fashion, that is, the same direction as the racers, the bow person of the support boat will pit the bow paddler of the race boat and the stern will be handled similarly.

Many boat pit teams find it easier to be paddling upstream, toward the racers, when conducting the pit exchange. It is easier for the pit teams to spot their racing team as it approaches and then adjust their canoe position to be on line with the oncoming racing team. Even though they are not able to paddle along with their team during the hand off, "upstream" pit teams find that by facing the racers and being sure of the right position in the river, the exchange goes more smoothly. In the upstream method, the bow person in the support boat pits the stern person in the racing boat and the stern person of the support boat replenishes the bow racer.

When pitting from a boat, the pit teams should not allow themselves to be intimidated by an oncoming horde of hard-charging paddlers. As long as the pit crew is lined up essentially with the current, it is a very easy matter for the racing teams to go by. They should never, under any circumstances, pull sideways in front of an oncoming team or interfere in any way with another racing team. Counsel them to take their time and wait until the pack is past. There will be plenty of time to gather spent jugs and paddle back to shore.

> **Make sure that your pit crews know that they should not assist you in any way other than to provide food, water, paddles, etc. This means that a pit team person may not give the racers a push or do anything that would help the racing team's forward progress. It is also strictly forbidden for a boat pit team to paddle along in a method that would permit the racing team to ride their wake.**

The Finish

Every canoe race is going to have a finish line. Your position when you get there will largely be dictated by the strategy and techniques you have employed up to this point. If you are all alone, you need only continue to paddle across the line.

In many circumstances, you are going to be with one or more canoes. When this happens, you will want to win the finishing sprint that you know is coming. Here's how to do it. First, as you are approaching the finish line, try to be in a position where you are resting as much as possible. You don't want to be working hard, pulling two or three other canoes up to the line, only to have them sprint by you. So ride a little wake, rest as much as possible, take a drink, splash water on your face. In short, try to mentally and physically prepare yourself for the final maximum energy output in the race.

Next, remember that boat position will be key. If you have any hope of winning a finishing sprint, you do not want to be on the back wave of any canoe. You need to be in the lead position, out on a side wake, or out on your own in water undisturbed by the wakes of your competitors.

If you know that you don't have a blazing sprint, try to drop the other canoes before you get too close to the finish line. Do whatever you can possibly do to get out ahead and stay there. You may want to do this by going with a long and steady grinding attack or instead, by using a series of repetitive top-speed sprints. If you have any shallow water in the last part of the race, don't hesitate to use it to your advantage. In any case, make the other canoes work hard trying to get over your wake if they are going to get past you.

On the other hand, if you are the type of team that has good high-end speed for short periods of time, you will want to be waiting, wake riding as comfortably as possible in an attacking position. Get on the side wake, placing your canoe as far forward as possible. (You don't want to be too far back where a sudden attack can force you to eat waves.) Work to keep your canoe in a position approximately equal with the lead boat — and don't let your bow drift back farther than the bow paddler in the lead boat.

Photograph by Michael Moore

Work to keep your boat equal with the lead
boat as you prepare for a final sprint.

In a final sprint, timing is critical. Most often, the winner is the sprinting team that gets the jump and is able to maintain its speed to the finish. That's because very few teams can hang onto the wake of a boat that has the jump and still muster enough energy to come back and take the lead. So wait as long as you can — but not too long. If another team goes first, ride their side wake as effortlessly as you can, staying far forward. You've got to hope that the sprinting team will lose some of their edge and, when this happens, pour it on with every ounce of energy you have left.

Whatever method you use to finish the race, it is imperative that you maintain proper technique. If you let your technique deteriorate when you are tired and in your finishing sprint, your boat speed will invariably suffer. Keep your composure and your form. If you know what the strengths of your team are, maintain proper technique, and time your finishing sprint correctly. More often than not you will hit the finish line in front of your competitors.

Then go treat yourself to a delicious carbo-load drink!

Chapter 11

Downriver Racing
Living On The Edge

"Either I'm going to win or I'm going to swim."
Ralph Vincent

When most people think about paddling through rapids or whitewater, they conjure up images of multi-person rafts, kayaks and closed canoes, or ABS recreational hulls (rubber boats) filled with air bags. Clearly, these are the vehicles of choice for the beginning paddler who seeks only to survive the rapids or for the experienced paddler who wants to play and surf heavy water.

Yet whitewater is not alone the province of rafts, kayaks, and rubber boats. There is also a sport where daring paddlers push open canoes down rapid-filled rivers with one goal in mind — speed. And these canoes bear little resemblance to their recreational brethren. They are long, sleek hulls with bucket seats and foot-braces—racing hulls in every sense of the word. They carry little flotation and the margin for error is even smaller.

The paddlers of these skinny racing canoes must take on everything the river throws at them, including standing waves, rock gardens, big drops, and portages. Most importantly, they've got to do it all while paddling fast and remaining afloat. The fastest canoe will usually be one that has paddled closest to the edge of disaster without sinking. Welcome to the world of downriver racing.

What Is Downriver Racing?

Downriver racing is precisely what the name implies. It is a race "downriver" wherein the competitors take on every difficulty and obstacle that comes their way. including rapids, rocks, drops, and portages. Courses for downriver racing vary widely in length, but most often will be found in the five to fifteen mile range. A typical downriver race will take from forty minutes to over two hours.

Courtesy of Cindy Lynch

In downriver racing, the team with the fastest line often wins—"it is as simple as that."

Unlike marathon racing where there are mass starts according to class, downriver competitors will usually start one at a time at intervals of about a minute. There are no packs and drafting almost never comes into play. Rather than focusing one's attention on the other competitors, the rigors of downriver racing force you to concentrate on the river itself. In the most immediate sense, it comes down to the paddlers versus the river. And like a bicycle time trial, a downriver race is a "race of truth." Each team must find its own course through the waves, the rocks, and the rapids. There are no gates or course markers. Each team paddles as close to the line of danger as possible, without flipping over or filling up with water. The team with the fastest time from point A to point B wins. It is as simple as that.

Downriver racing shares similarities with closed-canoe "wildwater" racing. The main difference lies in the fact that closed canoes, because they are "covered," do not take on water and may therefore go through much heavier rapids. In contrast, the open canoes of downriver racing are limited to a maximum of "Class four" rapids. Another difference is that the wildwater courses are generally much shorter, lasting twenty to twenty-five minutes. Endurance plays a much more significant role in downriver racing where the courses are substantially longer.

We have chosen to include a chapter on downriver racing in this book because the sport, as it has evolved, shares a great deal with modern marathon canoe racing. The paddling techniques are almost identical. The only real difference is that downriver racing naturally requires greater use of corrective strokes, such as draws, pries, and cross-draws, together with high and low braces. The canoes are very similar. Downriver racing canoes are little more than high-sided marathon canoes with a little flare to the hull. The seats and foot brace setups are the same. The canoe materials of choice are Kevlar® and Spectra® due to their toughness and light weight. But the most important characteristic shared by both forms of open boat racing is speed.

One of the first strokes the recreational whitewater paddler learns is the backpaddle, so the canoe can be slowed and maneuvered as it proceeds down a rapid. This helps the paddlers stay dry, and it provides an opportunity to make crucial route decisions. The backpaddle, however, is not in the downriver racer's repertoire. It is the speed factor which supplies the key ingredient that sets downriver open boat racing apart. Speed provides the thrills. Speed provides the spills. Speed provides the challenge. Many-time national champion Ralph Vincent likes to say the downriver paddler goes "full bore" into the teeth of heavy rapids.

When slashing through waves and souse holes at these speeds, it doesn't take long before you find that you are carrying a boatload of water. Only a paddler's technical skill and the ability to find and hold the canoe on subtle lines through the rapids stands in the way of a swim. Therein lies the special challenge of downriver racing.

A Bit Of History

Until the mid-1960's, the only kind of open canoes that paddlers used for downriver racing were traditional recreational canoes. These canoes were usually made out of aluminum or heavy fiberglass and they looked like what the average person perceives as a canoe. These canoes were big; they were heavy; they were dry. But they were also slow. People laughed at the idea of trying to go through heavy whitewater in a skinny, tippy racing canoe.

All this changed when a paddler from Jay, Maine, by the name of George Walsh, and his partner from Farmington, Maine, Ray Titcomb, went out to the Midwest to learn what the marathon racing canoes of the time were all about. They came back to New England with plans for a flatwater marathon racing canoe and used this as the basis of their new design for a whitewater racing hull. This canoe came out at 18-1/2 feet long and approximately 32 inches wide at the working waterline amidships. They raised the sides, making the hull deeper and added a little flare to help deflect big waves. After some other design alterations, this new whitewater racing canoe became known as the now famous "T.W. Special."

When George and Ray showed up with a racing hull at whitewater races, people were skeptical at best, and downright derisive at worst. No way could this skinny racing hull be put through difficult Class three and four rapids, said the critics. George Walsh and Ray Titcomb proved them wrong. In doing so, they also pioneered the use of marathon paddling technique, including calling "huts" and switching sides, in downriver racing. With their new boat and their new technique, not only did George and Ray make it down the whitewater courses, but they were winning by huge margins.

The Mad River Canoe Company bought the rights to produce the "T.W. Special," and the Sawyer Canoe Company quickly rose to the challenge with their downriver "Charger" model. Soon, Gene Jensen was designing whitewater racing boats, as were guys like Jim Henry, John MacDonald, Ted Bell, and others. The racing designs soon became more sophisticated; the layups became lighter and lighter. As the boats gradually became more fragile, it put a greater emphasis on technical skill.

Courtesy of Mad River Canoe

Modern downriver canoes are light and can fly down a moving river.

Today, there is very little difference between the look and the layup of a marathon racing canoe and a downriver racing canoe. The biggest difference is that the downriver canoe will be deeper and somewhat more stable. It will also be made with a layup that is a bit more rugged than found on today's ultralight marathon boats. Yet the modern downriver racing hulls can pick up and fly down a fast moving river. They are swift and they are fun to paddle.

Open boat downriver racing is popular throughout the country, but particularly in the Northeast and Southeast where the rivers provide plenty of Class two, three, and four whitewater. Most local races will have plenty of classes for recreational hulls and ABS boats so you don't need a racing canoe to get started. Once you get the bug, you will discover that the investment in a fast racing hull will be well worthwhile. Local and regional downriver races culminate in a National Downriver Championship which has been sponsored for many years by the American Canoe Association.

Equipment Considerations

The modern downriver racing canoe is a sophisticated speed machine designed to handle Class 2 chop to Class 4 drops with equal alacrity. At the working four-inch waterline, the hull shape of the downriver canoe looks very much like its marathon brethren. Above the waterline, however, you will find higher sides and substantial flair in the front portions of the canoe to deflect heavy waves and make the canoe as dry as possible when the bow plunges into heavy water. The bows and the sterns of these big racing canoes will usually be reinforced, as it is these two areas which take most of the beating.

The layups of downriver racers vary considerably. All the major manufacturers offer ultra light hulls made of Kevlar® or Spectra® combined with foam cores. These canoes are light and they are stiff, but they do not stand up to much of a pounding. If you are not an experienced whitewater racer this lightweight layup is not recommended.

The novice and intermediate paddler would do better with a heavier kevlar layup without the rigid foam core. Many manufacturers use a center rib and "pogo sticks" between the thwarts and the center rib to help keep the bottom stiff. These layups have substantially more give to them, and damage will be minimized upon impact with submerged rocks and logs. Although you give away some weight and some stiffness with the heavier layups, your canoe will be more durable. The choice is yours.

Speaking of choice, keep in mind that downriver racing still recognizes a so-called "short class" where the maximum length of the hull is 16 foot, 6 inches. These short canoes are a blast to paddle, particularly for racers on the smaller side. The short boats are more maneuverable than the 18-1/2 footers, but their reduced volume means that it is a particular challenge to keep them dry. They are fun and a thrill to paddle. Just ask George Walsh, the grand old man of downriver canoe racing, who has dominated this class for years.

The set-up of a downriver racing canoe is critical, but it is also a very individual matter. Ten years ago, a majority of downriver racers were still kneeling in their racing hulls on foam blocks or saddles. Today, the vast majority of racers sit in the canoes in classic marathon racing style.

> **The height of the seat is crucial to your stability. Hanging the seat low in the canoe increases stability, but it becomes somewhat more difficult to paddle over the high sides of the downriver racer. Raising the seat height improves your leverage and paddling position, but there is a significant trade-off in stability. If you are a beginner in the downriver racing scene, I recommend that you start with your seat low in the canoe, perhaps no more than six or seven inches off the bottom. You may raise your seat as your skill level and the particular downriver course dictate.**

In heavy water, you're going to need to be able to roll your gunnel down into the water and yet stay braced within the canoe. This means locking yourself into position. You and the canoe must be one. For the stern paddler, footstraps are a necessity. Many racers also utilize high sided "tractor" type seats to provide more support. In recent years, more and more paddlers have been using closed cell foam blocks glued to the inner sides of the canoe at the area of the hips and the knees so that the paddler is braced solidly within the canoe. (See photograph on next page.)

Do not neglect proper flotation. During a formal race, flotation is restricted by racing rules, usually to small airbags in the bow and stern. However, during any training run, I recommend that large airbags be utilized in the center of the canoe. Should the inevitable wipeout occur, the airbags will help float the canoe high in the water and assist in recovery and damage protection. A canoe without substantial flotation will ride low in the water once capsized and will very likely wrap around any obstacle it meets. There is nothing worse than buying a brand new downriver racing canoe only to wrap it around some rock or bridge abutment due to insufficient flotation.

Whitewater racing can be rough on paddles, too. While most experienced racers today are using the lightweight carbon fiber paddles, I recommend that people new to the sport use a medium-

Photograph by Peter Heed

A downriver setup as seen from the stern. Note the foam
blocks around the area of the hips.

weight carbon fiber blade, perhaps one with a Lexan tip. These
paddles will stand up much better when you pound them against
rocks. Many paddlers still go with wood paddles in downriver
racing and there is certainly a place for these paddles, particularly
in practice. Because it is easy to break and/or lose a paddle during
a race, <u>both</u> paddlers should have a spare secured in the canoe.

Most downriver races are of sufficient length to require drink
jugs. Be sure your jug is securely attached to the canoe. You will

want to glue a high-sided foam drink holder to the canoe bottom for your jug, and a little bit of added duct tape never hurts when it comes to keeping the jug where it belongs. A good many downriver races have been lost when a paddler goes to take a drink only to find that his jug has fallen out of the holder with all of his liquid draining into the bottom of the canoe.

Both paddlers should also have the availability of a hand-held bailer, usually in the form of a hard plastic "bleach-type" bottle with the bottom cut out. Self-bailers are not permitted in whitewater, so you are going to have to get rid of the water by hand. Depending on your trim, and the particular type of water you are in, the water to be bailed may be either in the stern or the bow, so both paddlers need to be ready with bailers. In the worst case scenario, the water may be several inches deep throughout the canoe, in which case both paddlers are going to want to bail like mad. The bailer can be affixed to the canoe with a string, with velcro, or with a foam clip arrangement which will hold the bailer secure to the canoe, ready when required.

Find The Fast Line

Finding the line down the river that is both fast and dry is what downriver racing is all about. If you ask ten downriver racers what the best line is down any river, you will probably get ten different answers. That's one of the aspects that makes downriver racing so much fun. There is no "right" answer. What is a good route for one paddler may not work for another paddler, and there are certainly routes which are inadvisable for all paddlers. You have to examine your own skills and be honest with yourself concerning your strengths and weaknesses. Many downriver racers will tend to be faster in the shallow chop and take somewhat conservative lines through the big rapids. Others may be slower in flatwater, but they make up for a lack of pure speed with consummate skill in running the heaviest drops and the fastest chutes.

It is safe to say that most rapids will usually offer a paddler three basic alternatives. The first will be a route that is relatively dry and safe, but somewhat slow. The intermediate route will carry with it increased risk of taking water, but will offer a faster line. The third alternative will be potentially the fastest but also the most dangerous. A wrong move in this route will mean not only taking a boatload of water, but perhaps a dump which could end your race.

Photograph by Tricia Heed

The fastest route may also be the most dangerous. Dick Weber and Jim Mallory show how its done.

Keep in mind that constantly running routes which put water into your canoe will not result in fast times as you will spend too much time bailing. To be fast, you must also be dry. It is the racers who can find the fastest possible current, without spending an inordinate amount of time bailing and without wiping out, who usually end up winners. Perennial national champions like New York's Dick Weber and Eric McNett, North Carolina's Bunny

Johns, and Virginia's Randy Drake and Nancy Shelhorse, are all geniuses at running beautiful, sophisticated lines through heavy whitewater. These racers are consistently able to find the fastest, driest routes and put their canoe where they want it to be. Other paddlers, such as Maine's Phil Soule, Michigan's George Stockman and Vermont's Ralph Vincent, have a reputation for simply going into the heaviest, fastest water they can find. Phil Soule calls it going "Cro-Magnon."

Photograph by Tricia Heed

Ralph Vincent shows why he is known for going "full-bore" into the heaviest, fastest water he can find.

One thing is clear. To be successful, you are going to need to scout the route you will want to paddle in heavy whitewater. This means you need to get to the race ahead of time so that you can preferably pre-run the course, or at least scout the worst rapids from the bank. The best way to scout is to run the river in your canoe, eddying out above big rapids and scouting from shore. Then run through the rapid on the line you have chosen. You can probably find an eddy at the bottom of the rapid in which to stop and analyze the pros and cons of the route you have just tried. Once you are confident of your line through that particular rapid, proceed downriver, going through the same procedure at the next difficult section.

There are no hard and fast rules governing route selection. No two rapids are alike — the complexion of any one particular rapid changes dramatically depending on water level. And for a given situation, it is common to find that two equally competent downriver paddlers choose to run the same rapid in different ways. So each paddler has to weigh the risk of any particular line through heavy water against the benefits of speed that may be gained if the line is run correctly. Each person must also factor in his or her preferences and strengths as a paddler into the mix. There are few constants in this game of speed through rapid-strewn rivers, but there are certain guidelines which may help you make the right decisions when searching for that fast line through the rapids.

Courtesy of We-no-nah Canoe Company

An open C-1 canoe running the shoulder of big standing waves.

In general, always be looking for tongues of fast-moving, non-aerating water. The telltale downstream "V" will often indicate to you the deepest and fastest moving water. Avoid slamming your bow into aerated souse holes or huge standing waves. These holes are fun for the playboat crowd to surf in but they do not help your downstream speed and can often lead to a boatload of water.

When it is necessary to run through a line of waves, you should search for a line midway between the top-most crest of the waves and the "valley" where the waves originate. This is known as running the "shoulder" of big waves. If you run right down the center of a field of standing waves, your canoe will be hammered by a series of blows as your bow smashes into each oncoming wave. This slows downriver speed. If you avoid the wave field altogether, you may find yourself crossing an eddy line into either slow-moving water or an upstream back eddy. The fast route is to run down on the shoulder of the standing waves.

It's also important to keep in mind that while rocks are obviously obstacles to be avoided, you do not need to miss them by much. You will often find fast tongues and currents of water squeezing through fairly tight spots between large boulders. In such cases, shooting the tongue by just missing the rock, (sometimes actually "kissing" it with your gunnel as you speed by), is the fastest way to go.

When you squeeze by a boulder, expect a severe eddy line on the backside of the boulder with slow-moving or upstream-moving water within the eddy. Avoid crossing this eddy line at all costs. Keep your canoe, and most importantly the bow of the canoe, in the fast-moving current outside of the eddy.

Severe eddies often form on the inside of tight turns of a relatively small whitewater river. Here again, it is often fastest to ride the swift current just outside of the eddy line, but under no circumstances allow the boat to cross into the eddy. Riding on fast water just outside an eddy line is much easier in a C-2 than in a C-1, for the C-2 team has the luxury of being able to keep a paddler on either side of the canoe, holding the canoe on line. It is also an advantage to have the paddlers near the ends of the canoe, providing better leverage and control. A C-1 downriver racer has to be more circumspect in how close he or she comes to a severe eddy line. If you are unfortunate enough to have your canoe caught by a sharp eddy line, you will need to be prepared for the quick 180° turn which will surely take place. Paddlers will need to brace and keep the boat level or even leaning to the downstream side as you spin. The canoe will have a tendency to pull down toward the upstream side, and this can lead to a quick swim in the eddy. Keep the boat rolled to the downstream side and stay braced.

As soon as you have stabilized, execute an eddy peel-out, turning downstream again. You will find that these big racing boats execute eddy turns fairly well, despite their length and lack of rocker. On the peel-out, again be wary of the tendency of the upstream gunnel to be pulled down by the current. The paddlers should lean toward the downstream side and maintain solid braces as they come out of an eddy. A quick recovery and peel-out after crossing into an eddy will help you limit your time loss to 30 seconds or less.

In corners of medium to large size whitewater rivers, you will often find the fastest route somewhere between the inside to the middle of the river. Although your natural inclination is to look for the fastest water on the outside of turns, you will often find quick water tongues on the inside which enable you to cut the corner without getting into any eddies. After you are through the turn, run the current back to the middle or outside to pick up the swift water.

This inside line, known as "dropping through the corner," is not only a fast line, but it is in most circumstances the safest line. Heavy standing waves and holes tend to build up on the outside of the turns — sure swampers. By riding the inside of the turn, along the inner edge of these big waves, you not only go fast but stay dry. Virginia's Charlie Barton is among the best at finding the good inside lines on whitewater rivers. Especially in his C-1, Charlie knows how to go fast and stay dry by dropping through the corner.

One other general guideline about fast lines: often the best line is a fairly straight one. While the fastest chutes may be alternatively on the right and then the left side of the river, your overall time will suffer if you have to spend too much time zig-zagging to reach these chutes. It is often better to find a relatively straight line through the rapid, even if it means not hitting the fastest tongue of water every time. There is much to be said for going straight and going fast, with as few corrective strokes as possible.

Hitting Your Chosen Line

It's one thing to scout out the perfect line through heavy water, it's another thing to actually execute the plan by hitting the line you have chosen. Execution depends upon a mixture of strength, speed, and anticipation. From a technique standpoint, you will want to be using standard marathon stroke technique as much as possible — probably 95% of the time. On the other hand, there comes times in whitewater when you simply have to move the big boat left or right and you have to do it <u>now</u>. Last second moves are accomplished with a combination of draws, cross-draws, pries and braces. Yet these strokes impede forward progress and should only be used as a last resort.

> **Just as in marathon racing, use radical corrective strokes when needed, but try to anticipate and make small corrections, keeping the power on the boat. In most circumstances, modern racing hulls respond to power strokes more readily than to sharp adjusting strokes. That is, whenever possible it is better to move the boat from one position in the river to another position in the river by power strokes which maintain some forward component. These strokes include, beside the basic forward stroke, quarter-drawing, and sweeping. If these power strokes don't put you where you want to be, then you must go to a full corrective stroke such as a draw or a pry.**

As in marathon racing, each paddler in downriver has individual responsibilities. The stern person is responsible for keeping the canoe on the general course in the river and for throwing in that last minute low brace to prevent disaster. The stern paddler has a broader perspective on matters, and often has a better opportunity to utilize the brace to prevent the canoe from going over. The stern person must also constantly seek to simply keep the stern of the boat in line behind the bow paddler, so that the smallest possible target is presented to oncoming rocks and obstructions. Finally, just as in marathon racing, the stern person must paddle in synch with the bow paddler.

Photograph by Tricia Heed

The stern paddler sometimes has to throw in a quick brace to prevent disaster.

The bow person, who has a better view of what is immediately in front of the canoe, sets the stroke pace and is responsible for quick changes in direction. This translates into making sure that the bow misses obstructions and is often cause for dramatic last second corrective strokes, moving the boat either left or right. A glancing blow on a rock as the boat slides by is not a serious problem, but a head-on "bus stop" of a boulder can ruin your whole day. Thus the bow person must paddle aggressively and be decisive in difficult situations. Once the bow paddler makes a move, the stern person must get the boat in line and follow.

Good teamwork is essential. When mistakes are made and obstructions hit, as they inevitably will be, there can be no time for blame or recriminations. Both paddlers must continue to focus on their individual jobs and continue to anticipate the river ahead. Setting a canoe up on the right line in advance of trouble is half the battle — this takes consistent cooperation and teamwork.

The Big Drops

You've made it past the standing waves, the severe eddy lines, and the rock gardens. Now it's make or break it time. The river seems to disappear up ahead. It's time for the big drop. It's time to pray to the River God.

The names alone of the big drops on some of the most famous downriver courses speak volumes about the challenge they present. "Satan's Kingdom" on the Farmington River; "Cucumber" on the Youghiogheny; "Nantahala Falls" on the Nantahala River; "Spencer's Rips" on Dead River; "The Gorge" on the Westfield; the "Dumplings" on the West River; and "Railroad Rapid" on the Esopus are a few names that conjure up exciting memories for experienced paddlers and will pump up the heart rate of any true downriver racer.

How do you handle the big drop in an open racing boat? The first thing to remember is that there is a time to slow down in downriver racing — and it is now. The problem in the big drops is often how to keep your bow from submerging in the aerated water at the bottom of the drop. Slowing down helps prevent the bow from diving and gives the flared hull of the boat a chance to work.

> **Most drops have one or more good tongues of solid current coursing over them and racers should attempt to place their boat on such a tongue. These tongues are much easier to see from below a rapid than from above, so when scouting the rapid beforehand, try to line up the correct tongue with a tree or other object in the distance which will help put you on the right line when approaching from upriver. Don't come into a big drop "blind."**

If the drop is particularly big and severe, racers should consider shifting their weight back in the canoe, creating a momentary bow-light situation. This is most easily accomplished by having the bow paddler slide back a foot or more toward the rear of the canoe. Some bow paddlers are known to kneel behind the bow seat in an attempt to shift their weight and bring their center of gravity as low as possible. It also puts them in an optimum position to "pray to the River God." The stern paddler can also move back, but the effect of this upon the canoe will not be as dramatic.

Photograph by Tricia Heed

Hitting a big drop. Note the bow paddler drawing the boat to run the best line.

The approach to a few big drops will require the paddlers to power into their line in order to place the canoe in the proper location. The more typical approach, however, calls for slowing the canoe down somewhat, allowing it to slide through the drop while taking on a minimum of water. As the bow of the canoe approaches the base of the drop, the bow person should throw out a strong low brace, helping to lift the bow out of the hole and prevent water from pouring in. Court McDermott is fond of calling this very effective technique the "drop and plop."

Even when doing the "drop and plop," the stern will have a tendency to slam into the rock ledge that often lurks at the bottom of big drops, so it is important for the stern person to anticipate this with a timely low brace. In all events, as the paddlers proceed over any drop, both racers should avoid making any last second changes or switching of sides — suddenly having both paddlers on the same side is a quick recipe for a swim.

Getting The Water Out — In A Hurry

So, you made it over the big drop just as you planned but that big roller at the bottom hammered you pretty hard and your boat took on water. If it's just a small amount of splash, don't worry about it; paddle on. But if you took too much and have an inch of water or so sloshing around either end of the canoe, it's time to bail.

Leaving that much or more water in your canoe is a sure way to draw trouble. It's not just the fact that the water adds weight to the canoe, but rather the fact that it is <u>moving</u> weight that causes the problem. The accumulated water will slosh around in the canoe, proceeding from back to front or side to side, wreaking havoc with your balance and momentum.

> **Ever try pulling off an eddy turn or other sharp maneuver carrying a boatload of water? I don't recommend it. The water carries with it a momentum all its own which resists any change of course. You turn the canoe one way, the water goes another way, and the result is a quick swim. So go to the bailer as soon as you take on significant water.**

If you have a real boatload of water, there will be little choice but for both racers to stop paddling and start bailing. This is slow, but it is better than going downriver into the next drop full of water. A better method, instead of stopping, is to try to get the water forward in the canoe so that the bow paddler can bail while the stern person paddles. The stern person will be able to keep the boat going straight and you will lose very little time overall. To get the water to run to the bow, some teams simply have the bow person move forward, although this can restrict your bailing area. Most teams find that it is best for the stern person to get off his seat and kneel a few feet forward in the canoe. The stern person can then proceed to paddle from this position while the bow person bails the water that has run forward. As soon as the canoe is relatively dry, both paddlers resume their usual positions and hammer down the river.

> **If the water in your canoe is more than 3 or 4 inches deep, you may have no choice but to pull over to river's edge and dump the water out. This should be a last resort for it results in a huge loss of time. So, if possible, crank up those hand bailers and "keep on truckin'."**

Junk Water And Chop

Whitewater rivers tend to be, by their nature, fairly shallow. Most downriver courses therefore will be characterized by a significant amount of one to three foot deep "junk water." Racers will also find many stretches of shallow Class 1 and 2 standing waves, known as "chop." These stretches on downriver courses provide an opportunity for experienced marathon paddlers to shine.

Courtesy of We-no-nah Canoe Company

Stretches of shallow Class 1 and 2 standing waves provide opportunities for experienced paddlers to shine.

The paddling technique for these sections of junk water and chop is almost precisely the same technique used by marathon paddlers in shallow water (See chapter 8). The racers will want to bring their boat to top hull speed by sprinting forward with a relatively short, quick stroke. Just as in everyday shallow water, it is important to increase the canoe's speed prior to entering the shallow water so you can keep the hull up and surfing on the shallow water wave. Yes, even these big downriver boats will pop up and plane shallow whitewater and chop.

As in marathon racing, the trim of your canoe is crucial. But, unlike marathon racing, where you've usually already trimmed for shallow water, you may find yourself coming downriver into chop and junk water at less than optimal trim. That's because on heavy whitewater rivers, many teams run level boat trim or slightly bow-light to keep their boats dry. So you will need to get your bow down in shoal water and chop, and the best way to probably do this is by moving the bow person forward. Anticipate just as you do in shallow water — put your canoe in a bow-down trim <u>before</u> you enter the shoal and chop water sections. Then sprint your canoe up to speed and show how these whitewater boats can really fly.

Going For A Swim

If you paddle whitewater for any length of time at all, there are sure to be those occasions where you will find yourself out of the canoe and in the river. Whether your canoe has capsized or simply taken on so much water that it sinks, you need to know how to cope with the unpleasant experience of swimming through a rapid. Of primary consideration always will be your own safety and recovery. Secondarily, you will want to take the proper steps to recover your canoe.

At the outset it goes without saying that you should not be racing in downriver whitewater races unless you are a strong swimmer with no fear of water. Additionally, you should never go without wearing a buoyant PFD (personal flotation device). A properly worn PFD allows you to safely swim through rapids and provides you with the extra margin of safety that permits time to recover canoes, paddles, etc. Finally, if the water is cold, you should be properly outfitted in a wetsuit.

When your canoe sinks or capsizes, your first thought should be to stay with the canoe as long as it is practical. Move to the upstream end of the canoe, and hold on to the grab loop or painter. This will help keep the canoe straight as it works its way down through the rapids. When possible, you should attempt to pull the upstream end of the canoe towards shore or into an eddy where recovery will be possible. Most racers find that they will instinctively hold onto their paddle. If you have lost your paddle, you should be able to utilize the spare secured within the canoe.

Once you are safely to shore or in a calm eddy, roll the water out of the canoe and scramble aboard. Bail the remaining water, and head downriver. Many a downriver race has been won by a team which has taken a swim but made a quick recovery. Keep in mind that on difficult rivers, many teams may very well end up doing their best imitation of a submarine. So whether or not you are in contention, try to bring your boat in and finish as long as you can do so safely.

> **No matter how big the race, the paramount consideration is your own personal safety. There will be other races and other canoes. Never jeopardize your own personal safety or the safety of others in an unreasonable attempt to save a canoe. If you come upon another racer in trouble, you must immediately stop and render assistance.**

Here are some guidelines for getting out of trouble in dangerous conditions:

1. If due to the violence of an approaching rapid or because of the cold temperature of the water, you are in greater danger staying with the canoe, then leave it and head for shore.

2. Never allow yourself to end up on the downstream side of a canoe where you can be pinned between it and an obstacle such as a rock or log.

3. When you find yourself swimming through a rapid

on your own, try to lie on your back with your feet leading the way downriver. You can maneuver with your arms and let your feet and legs absorb any collisions with rocks.

4. Do not try to stand up in fast moving water unless it is so shallow that you cannot swim.

Winning Downriver Races

There is no magic formula that will guarantee your success in downriver racing. Winning will require a combination of physical conditioning, technical skills, whitewater sense, and the proper mental attitude. Of these, mental attitude often is the difference between winners and losers. Downriver racing throws a continuing barrage of challenges at the paddler. Because of the ceaseless difficulties encountered during any downriver race, finding and running the correct line 100 percent of the time is nearly impossible. I frankly know of no paddler who has ever had a "perfect" run.

Things will go wrong. You may not hit a line just right, or you may take on water where you never thought you would and find that submerged rock that lurked just below the surface and was impossible to see. Whatever the obstacles and difficulties, they must be continuously met and overcome with an aggressive and positive mental attitude.

With drops, chutes, and rocks coming at you in rapid-fire succession, there is no time to think about or assess blame for why your canoe took on water at the last set of standing waves or why you may have missed your line through the previous rock garden. Successful downriver racers have to keep putting their problems behind them and focus on the upcoming challenges.

Two downriver paddlers I recently observed on Maine's Dead River best exemplify the positive, slightly crazy mental outlook of a good downriver racer. I was sitting on a rock near the bottom of Poplar Hill Falls watching teams practice for the next day's race. Two fellows that I did not recognize were working their way down the technical left side of the rapid, when somebody appeared to miss a stroke and their racing canoe capsized within a blink of the eye. An overturned hull and two heads bobbed down through

Photograph by Tricia Heed

Along with the drops, chutes, and rocks, you never know what other obstacles you'll encounter in downriver racing!

mammoth standing waves. The paddlers did not appear to be in jeopardy, but they could not prevent their canoe from taking a crushing broadside blow from a pyramid-shaped rock. The canoe and paddlers were washed over three more big drops before they finally were able to get the canoe into an eddy very near where I was sitting. The racers struggled to roll the water out of the canoe, only to find that the left gunnel had been shattered and the kevlar ripped. Still, they managed to climb aboard and bail like mad. They gave no thought to quitting, and as they pointed their battered racer downriver, the bow person turned around and yelled, "Ain't this fun!"

Those two fellows had obviously discovered what all downriver racers know: the thrills and the spills that go along with racing open downriver canoes through whitewater provide about as much fun as a paddler can have.

Chapter 12

Canoe Triathlons

"Tri and Tri Again"
Triathlon team name

Many people first become exposed to marathon canoe racing through watching or participating in a canoe triathlon. These run, bike, and canoe events (not always in that order) are some of the more interesting athletic "happenings" of the racing season. The mix of road racing and canoe sprints in a relay format is exciting for participants and spectators and draws big crowds. For example, The Great Race, held every August in Auburn, New York, draws nearly 600 four-person teams. On the west coast, Eppie's Great Race, billed as the World's Oldest Triathlon, has over 1,700 competitors. In northern ski country, triathlons are occasionally expanded to quadrathlons, with a cross country ski leg added, and a mountain bike route for the cycling segment, to produce early spring larks for adventurous competitors.

Canoe triathlons range in size from several dozen teams to "mega" events. Most have categories for four-person teams as well as ironpersons, and more and more are adding two-person and three-person classes. Regardless of race size and location, there's always a need for good canoe racers.

Finding a Triathlon Team

Racing canoes and experienced paddlers are prized commodities on triathlon teams. Runners and cyclists seem to be a dime a dozen but competent canoeists are scarce — especially to non-paddlers trying to put teams together. Quite often, just in order to put together a team and get entered in the race, a runner and a biker will recruit a couple of friends to borrow a canoe and do the canoe leg. These teams usually do quite well in the run leg and the bike segment but the canoe crew is the weak link — frequently the canoe partners will be logging a certain amount of "on-the-job" training as they complete the canoe leg. So, there's a great need for canoe racers on triathlon teams and it's a fine low key way to break into canoe racing.

Most triathlons, even the small ones, have a variety of classes. One of the tricks in putting together a team is to look at the race categories and try to fit into one where you'll be competitive. (For example, avoid the open male category unless you're a fast paddler with a 30-32 minute 10K runner and a like-gifted cyclist.) Take a look at the mixed and masters categories. John Ayer, a 72-year old canoeist, paddles with Herm Schlimmer who is also over 70. They often recruit a runner and a cyclist who are in their 20's to round out the team. This mixture gives them an average age to fit into the "over-40" class and they end up being very competitive. Check the rules, not all races allow this age-blending. (In a 1990 triathlon, Ayer teamed up with three other men over 70. *Team 284* —the sum of their ages — not only beat half the field but won their 50+ age group.)

Paddling a two-person canoe can be, as we mentioned before, an ongoing course in human relations. There is no "captain" in a C-2 racing canoe and you've got to get along to go along. And while getting along with your canoe partner is an important part of working together as a team over a training and racing season, add two more people to the equation, and you have the potential for real human drama. Not long ago, canoeist Steve Wightman and his partner were planning on being a top-five team in a big race. They learned, minutes before the start, that their runner had gotten into a spat with his girl the night before and had decided not to show up. They recruited a local runner on the spot and managed to race — grumbling all the way to a middle-of-the-pack finish. Teams may have paddles break, canoes overturn, cyclists blow tires, or runners poop out, but most, in spite of pre-race calamities ("Weren't you supposed to bring the life jackets?") will have a happy reunion after the race and be ready to make plans for the next team triathlon.

Photograph by Dick Mansfield

Canoe racers are in demand for triathlon teams.

Since canoe triathlons feature short canoe segments, why not use them as anaerobic threshold training speed workouts?

As a canoe racer, you will find that your talents (and your canoe) are in demand for team triathlons. Once you get a team together that is reliable and fun to work with, you'll tend to stay together. Many canoe tri teams have raced together for five to ten years. If you like to run or bike, you may want to give a two-person team a try or, with solo paddling, do the event as an ironperson. Regardless of which mode you choose, triathlons are guaranteed fun for the beginner or the pro — short races with lots of competition and drama. They are a great way to break into canoe racing.

Photograph by Carl Caylor

Triathlon canoe courses are short so it is "bust it" time.

The Team Canoe Leg

There are no standard sequences for team triathlons although generally the canoe leg is last. Regardless of whether the canoes go first or last, you are likely to find yourself on the water with a strange variety of craft. You may be side-by-side with a fiberglass recreational canoe manned by a couple of football players or be waking with a fast-moving carbon boat. In a small race, you may be alone. This variety adds spice to the water leg of canoe triathlons.

In triathlons where the canoes go first, the race becomes much more like a regular canoe race except that all classes go at once. The faster teams get off the line rapidly while the rest play "dodge-'em" with one another. In a race like the Josh Billings, where there are two laps, there is an added element of excitement when the faster craft have to weave there way through the pack on the second lap.

The most common sequence for triathlons is a run leg, then a bike leg, and lastly, the canoe leg. You will have all sorts of time to wait before "strutting your stuff." You can watch the run, watch your cyclists head out, and then anxiously wait, hoping for no flat tires or crashes, until it's your turn. Usually, one of the canoeists has to run from the changeover zone to the canoe and off you go on a short fast canoe leg. If you are up with the leaders, you will be dueling with good canoeists, probably teams that you've raced before. Because it's such a short course, there's little time for a lot of strategy. It's "bust it" time. Grab a side wake if you can and use the buoy turn to your advantage. If you are further back in the race, there is often a good chance to pick up a lot of places. Many teams in the middle of the pack will have unskilled paddlers and slow boats. Canoe legs are between 4 and 7 miles in most races so it is just a matter of hard, efficient paddling. Watch out for collisions and have fun, for it will be over before you know it.

Ironperson Triathlons

Many canoe triathlons allow you to compete as an ironperson. Aside from the obvious challenges of doing the whole race yourself, there are other reasons that individuals are attracted to do a canoe triathlon solo. You may not own a C-2 or have a partner. You may be a runner or cyclist who doesn't like swim triathlons. You may just like cross-training — quite a few cross-country ski racers do tri's by themselves. Or you may be a canoeist who doesn't especially like to run, enjoys biking a bit more, and loves to paddle. Once you get through the first two legs, you're happy — and ready to move up some places on the water.

The equipment that most triathletes lug to races is expensive and high tech. While you can get started with an older 10-speed bike and recreational canoe, you'll soon be frustrated and eyeing the faster equipment, especially as it passes you in the race. John Aufmuth, who won the USCA Masters Triathlon in 1990, in talking about his equipment said, "At our age, we buy speed." He's right. Most ironpersons buy the best gear that they can afford.

Getting Set Up

Doing a canoe triathlon by yourself takes some planning. First, use a checklist to make sure everything is loaded in or on the car when you are ready to go. Get to the race early to get the canoe and bike placed. If you have a crew person to help with your gear, all the better. As with any race, you should study the race instructions. Most are standard — you must wear a regulation helmet for the cycling and you must have a PFD for each canoe occupant. Check the instructions for drafting on the bike leg — is it allowed or not? Check the direction of the turn around the buoy in the canoe leg? Observe how they want the race numbers attached to the bike and canoe.

Find out where the bike will go and get it set up. Lay out your helmet and shoes. Don't count on a bike rack although some races have them or there may be a rope that you can tie the bike to. You can bring a triangle bike stand, like those used in a bike shop, or just use an old plastic bucket turned upside down, upon which the pedal rests. The bucket can be used to lug your water, towels, gloves, bike shoes, and hard hat. Arrange your gear so that you can sit down after the run, get your gear on, get a drink, and get on your way. After a few triathlons, you'll have your system down pat.

> **You'll have to get used to leaving expensive equipment by itself if you ironperson. If you have an expensive carbon fiber paddle, you may be reluctant to leave it in the canoe but most ironpersons do. Good race directors have marshalls watching the equipment during and after the race. With a crew person, you eliminate the stolen equipment anxiety and can focus your tensions on the race.**

The canoe setup is simpler since all you do is put the PFD in the canoe, set up the drinking system, and store your extra paddle. If the first event is the run, get all the preparation done at least 30 minutes before the start and start focusing on the first event, warming up and hydrating.

The Run Leg

Whether coming first or last in the race, the run is the leg that many canoeists dread. On the other hand, it is the portion where newcomers to canoeing, especially if they come from a running background, can pick up time. The length for run leg of a triathlon is normally from 5 to 7 miles with 10K being a popular distance. The courses are usually flat and fast.

As in any race, make sure that you start off well-hydrated. You have a 2-3 hour session ahead and probably will be doing some of it in hot humid conditions. Watch the other ironpersons. You'll see them lugging a water bottle with them as they warm up. If you plan to use a sports drink on the bike and in the canoe, sip it as you get ready to run. Warm up easily and get ready to race.

Photgraph by Carl Caylor

You can gain during triathlon transitions by being well-organized and efficient.

If the run is first, you will be off in a large pack, as in any running race, but remember, most of your companions may be only running the first leg (they are the runner for a four person team) so don't get carried away with the pace. You can check numbers as you run along — the ironpersons usually have a number on the back or side as well as the front. Even though you have two more events ahead, run your normal race pace. There's not a lot of reason to hold back — you can recover on the bike. Take fluids at the water stops and work at maintaining a steady pace. The transition is a place where you can pick up a little time by being well-organized and efficient. Have extra fluids ready and gulp them as you change shoes, don your helmet and gloves, and take off with care. In hot weather, a container of clear water is great to splash over the head as you transition.

Many iron persons use "platforms" on their clip-on peddles so that they can cycle in their running shoes. On a flat bike course where cycling shoes are not crucial, this can save a lot of time in transitions at the start and the end of the cycling leg.

If the run is last, you'll transition from the bike or the boat. Tank up from your water bottle as you near the finish and take more fluids as you drop your bike, change shoes, and head out. You'll find the first half mile a little wobbly after biking. Work at running smoothly and little by little, your legs will adjust and soon you should be running normally. Again, take fluids and maintain a steady pace. The race will be strung out by now but you should have, if you are a decent runner, some runners up ahead to try to pick off. Try to maintain good form and keep a steady pace to the finish line.

The Bike Leg
The cycling leg of most canoe triathlons is between 15 and 25 miles. Most ironpersons use a light road bike with some aerodynamic enhancements such as aero bars — they not only reduce drag but they can help you relax your arms. Disk wheels are common

Photograph by Peter Heed

The run to bike transition in a team triathlon is exciting for spectators.

Photograph by Carl Caylor

Ironpersons drop their expensive canoes and paddles quickly after the canoe leg of the triathlon.

among serious triathletes. It is not unusual to pay over $800 for a competitive bike — plan to get the lightest, fastest bike that you can afford.

> **One good way to get a feeling for what people are using is to walk up and down the bike racks before a race. You will not only see some interesting equipment, you also will learn more about how to store your gear, set up your drinking system, or even store your helmet and gloves.**

Several of the books listed in the Resources section have excellent write-ups of the cycling segment. Rather than cover cycling training and technique in detail, we refer you to those sources. Keep in mind that these descriptions are aimed at swim triathletes who swim first, then bike, then run.

Canoe ironpersons, who generally run first, face a different situation. You'll find that even if you are dead tired from the run, you can recover nicely on the bike, taking fluids and getting your pulse back to a lower level. Experienced triathletes recommend taking it easy the first few miles, spinning in a lower gear and getting the legs accustomed to cycling.

It is possible that you will encounter some leg cramping when you are well into the bike leg. This can occur with little warning — you are going along fine and suddenly someone takes a vise grip to your calf and you may have to stop. The way to prevent cramps is to keep the fluid level up in your body and train the body to do the run/bike transition. Many ironpersons will do a five mile tempo training run and then hop on their bike for a workout, getting the legs used to the transition. Others concentrate on stretching the calf muscles when they cycle by standing up on the hills and spinning easily during the initial biking. For most canoe triathletes, the bike leg is a good recovery period after the run and leaves them ready to take on their specialty, solo paddling.

Some canoe triathlons allow drafting on the bike segment so if that is the case, try to work with others in a pace line. What you'll find is that some races prohibit drafting and so state in the race directions — others just don't mention it. In the latter cases, when you see racers forming small packs, jump aboard.

Be methodical in replacing fluids, drinking from your water bottle at regular intervals. Change your riding position periodically, moving your hands from the drops, to the brake levers, to the aero bar — just to keep loose. As in the run, be smooth and efficient and relaxed as you experience what is for many, the most enjoyable part of the event.

Be careful entering the changeover zone and take a few seconds to set your expensive bike down and remove your hard hat and gloves as you jog off to the canoe. In some races it is quite a little run so you may opt for light sneakers or some type of foot protection. The hardy types kick off their bike shoes and run barefoot — wincing all the way.

The Canoe Leg

We have already talked about C-1 canoe racing so what is new here? First of all, in the run, bike, canoe sequence you will be tired, especially in the lower extremities, and you may find some new aches and pains in the legs as you canoe.

> **Because you will be in a mixed group of boats, your ability to wake ride (draft) will help significantly. As you come up on slower moving canoes, jump the stern and/or side wake, pausing momentarily to rest and lower your heart rate. If a faster C-1 or C-2 comes by, do not miss the opportunity to jump on the wake and get pulled up through the crowd. Good wake riding skills can help you improve your position significantly.**

But the biggest difference will probably be your racing companions on the water — you may well find yourself in a "demolition derby." Many tri teams, especially those comprised of younger athletes, often have a high school runner and a quick cyclist. Then they get a couple of wrestlers, or their current dates, to make up the rest of the team. If you are a novice ironperson, you may "hit the water" with this bunch of over-eager paddlers driving their ABS and aluminum behemoths hard — in many directions. This adds some excitement to your last leg as well as a chance to pass quite a few entrants.

Photograph by Carl Caylor

Skilled canoe racers "eat up"" the canoe leg of triathlons.

As mentioned, canoe legs are between 4 and 7 miles in most races and often call for a buoy turn. They normally do not involve shallow water or tricky currents. The triathlon is now a canoe sprint, so it's a matter of hard efficient paddling. Keep the fluids going; use your back muscles instead of your arms. Concentrate on good paddling technique and you will finish the triathlon feeling strong.

Glossary

ACA   American Canoe Association.

Aerobic   Training "with oxygen" at a pace within the training heart rate.

Aerobic Capacity   The ability to supply oxygen to the muscle tissues.

Anaerobic   Training "without oxygen." Also called oxygen debt.

Backpaddle   Paddling backwards (e.g., to hold a canoe on the start line).

Bailer   A device in the bottom of the canoe which extracts water when the boat is moving.

Bar   Shallows, usually with sand or gravel, found on the inside bend of a curve in the river.

Beam   The width of a canoe at its widest point.

Blade   The flat portion of the paddle.

Bonk   To become exhausted during competition — usually because of lack of fluids and/or nutrients.

Brace   A stroke used to stabilize canoe — may be a high brace or low brace.

Bridge   To close the interval between canoes.

Broach   Swinging broadside to the current or to waves.

Carbon fiber   A material used in racing paddles and boats.

Carry   Same as portage. A section where the canoe is carried on land.

Cavitation   Trapped air and disturbed water.

Catch   Planting the paddle in the water at the start of the forward stroke.

Center of Gravity   The center point of weight in a canoe.

Chair dip   A dip down between two chairs. Used to strengthen the arm muscles and shoulders.

Chine   The curved section of a canoe's side where it merges with the bottom.

Chop   Stretches of shallow Class 1 and 2 standing waves.

Chute   A fast-moving section of river, usually squeezed between two obstacles, such as pillars of a bridge.

Classification   The rating of rivers and streams, or sections of them, with regards to navigation. (Class 1 — moving water with a few riffles. Class 2 — Easy rapids up to 3 feet. Class 3 — Rapids with high, irregular waves with narrow passages. Classes 4, 5, & 6 are too hazardous for open canoes.

Comber   A big wave.

Confluence   Where two streams meet.

Cover   A fabric covering for racing canoes to protect them from ultraviolet rays and "road rash". Also a term used to describe the meeting of a challenge, e.g., to "cover" an attack.

Crest   The top of a wave or wake.

Cross-current   Water moving at an angle to the main flow.

Cross-training   Using a combination of activities for workouts. Running, cycling and weight training are an example.

Deck   Covered sections of canoes such as the middle of pro marathon boats.

Decked Canoe   Fully covered whitewater canoe.

Displacement   The volume of water displaced by a loaded canoe.

Downriver Race   A long distance race through whitewater.

Downstream Ferry   Backpaddling when the boat is angled to the current.

Draw Stroke   Pulling the canoe toward an anchored blade.

Drop   As in bicycle racing, to leave a canoe behind — usually by sprinting. Also refers to a significant change in river level, such as a ledge, in downriver.

Dry Pack   A waterproof bag for clothing and other items.

Ethafoam   Rigid foam used for bottle holders, spray rails and paddle holders.

Eddy   Sections of a river or stream where, due to obstructions or the shoreline, the current is reversed.

Eddy Line   The demarcation line between the main current and an eddy, sometimes marked by turbulence and small whirlpools.

Fartlek   "Speed play." Changing speeds during a speed workout.

Fast-twitch fibers   Muscle fibers that release glycogen rapidly.

Feather   Bringing the paddle forward edge-first during the recovery.

Feed   A drink for athletes such as defizzed cola, ERG, or MAX.

Ferry   To head the canoe across the stream angled so that the current hits the upstream side, moving the canoe across to the other shore.

Flotation   Buoyancy added to canoes for downriver racing.

Forward Stroke   The basic power stroke for canoeing.

Freeboard   The distance between the water and the gunnels.

Glycogen   The substance stored in muscles and used up in long races.

Grab Lines   Ropes attached to bow and stern for downriver. Same as painter.

Gunnel   Also called gunwale. The strips along the top edge of the canoe.

Heart monitor   A training device strapped across the chest which determines heart rate. Usually has a wristwatch display.

Hypothermia   A decrease in body temperature caused by exposure. A potentially serious problem when paddling early in the year.

Imagery   A "psyching" technique used to get ready to compete.

Intermediate water   Water which is between one foot and two to three feet in depth and therefore very difficult to paddle in.

Intervals   Speed work consisting of short spurts, usually repeated. Can be done in the canoe, on the bike, or by running.

J-stroke   A centering stroke used at the end of the forward stroke to keep canoe straight. Rarely used in canoe racing.

Jumping   Explosive acceleration consisting of all-out effort along with quicker and shorter strokes. The way you get your boat up on a wave.

Junk Water   Same as intermediate water.

Keel   A strip that runs from stem to stern along the bottom for reinforcement and stability. Rarely seen in racing boats.

Keel line   A line from bow to stern in the center of the hull. Used visually to switch strokes and to maintain a parallel stroke in marathon racing.

Kinesthetic sense   Awareness of what is happening to the body.

Lactic acid   The substance generated at a rate faster than the body can assimilate when athletes go anaerobic.

Lay-up   A term used for soaking fiberglass in resin — also used for newer materials.

Layering   Dressing in layers, usually three, for cold weather paddling. (Wicking, insulation, protection.)

Lean   Rolling the canoe on its side to help turn it.

Life Vest   Personal flotation gear, also called a "PFD."

Low Brace   A stabilizing stroke use with the paddle nearly flat on the water.

Masters   Canoe racers over 40.

Max VO2   A measure of the capacity of the oxygen system.

Mixed Teams   C-2 teams with a male paddler and a female paddler.

Off Side   The side of the boat you are not paddling on.

Oxygen debt   Going past the anaerobic threshold in exertion.

Paddle Poling   Driving paddle blades into the bottom of the river or lake and pushing the boat forward with a downward action of the upper arm in water that is extremely shallow — less than four to five inches deep.

Painter   A bow or stern line in a whitewater boat, also called a grab line.

Peel-out   Exiting from an eddy.

PFD   Personal Flotation Device.

Plyometrics   Lengthening a muscle (stretching it) before it contracts.

Pogo Sticks   Resilient supports used in downriver canoes to absorb shocks.

Poling   Moving a canoe, usually while standing, with a pole.

Popping   Same as jumping.

Port   The left side of a canoe.

Portage   Same as a carry.

Post   A maneuver by the bow paddler where a static brace is used to form a pivot point. Used for sharp turns. (Also called a high brace or a bow rudder.)

Power Face   The paddle face side that bears against the water.

Pry   Stroke that pushes the boat away from the paddle. Opposite from a draw.

Pulley   A simple way to strengthen arms. Most have variable resistance.

Recovery   The phase of the forward stroke where the paddle exits the water and is being brought forward for re-entry.

Riffles   Stretch of quick moving water with small waves, usually Class 1.

Rock Garden   A navigable boulder-strewn section of river.

Rocker   The sweep of the keel from the center to the bow or stern. Marathon canoes have little rocker — downriver boats have a lot for maneuverability.

Roller skis   Short skis with rubber-tired wheels use to practice cross country skiing in off-season.

Ruddering   Using the paddle as a rudder.

Seniors   Paddlers over 50 years of age.

Shallow Water   Water less than one foot deep.

Skateblades   Plastic molded hockey skates with 3 to 5 small in-line wheels popular for ski skating practice.

Sides   Where both paddlers are paddling on the same side. Used for some turns and in unusual wind conditions.

Slalom   A whitewater course with gates.

Slow-twitch fibers   Muscle fibers which utilize glycogen efficiently during long duration exercise.

Souse Holes   A depression in a river surface resulting in turbulent sections full of frothy aerated water.

Specificity   Training aimed at developing skills and muscles for a particular sport. The term used to denote that an exercise uses many of the same muscles as a given sport — i.e., paddling machines are specific to canoe racing.

Spray rails   Barriers added to the gunnels to help keep water out. Usually made of foam and either glued to canoe side or hooked over gunnel.

Standing Wave   A permanent wave caused by a submerged object.

Starboard   The right side of the canoe as you sit in it.

Strainer   A tree or similar obstruction through which water flows. Known to "eat" unwary canoes.

Stripper   A wood strip canoe (thin wood strips covered with fiberglass). Stiff, light, and reasonably-priced, they are popular in marathon racing.

Suck Water   Same as intermediate water.

Surfing   Riding downwind on the crests of large waves.

Swamp   When a canoe fills with water but does not capsize.

Sweep Stroke   A wider forward stroke used to help turn the canoe.

Thwart   A cross brace from gunnel to gunnel.

Training effect   The exercise level need to derive benefits, usually 60 to 70% of maximum heart rate.

Triathlon   An event combining running, and biking, and canoeing.

Trim   The balance, fore and aft and side to side, of a canoe on the water.

Trough   The depression between two waves.

Tumblehome   The curved sides of a canoe from the waterline to the gunnels.

Wake   To "draft" off another canoe. To ride one's wake.

Yoke   A padded device for carrying a canoe on portages.

Resources

Periodicals

American Whitewater   The bimonthly publication of the American Whitewater Affiliation

Bicycling   33 E. Minor St., Emmaus, PA 18098

Canoe   10526 N.E. 68th, Suite 3, Kirkland, WA 98033

Canoe and Kayak Racing News   P. O. Box 3146, Kirkland, WA. 98083

Canoe News   The bimonthly publication of the U.S. Canoe Association

Canoeing   Booklets published yearly by Ketter Canoeing, Minneapolis, MN

Paddler   P.O. Box 635, Oscoda, MI 48750

Runner's World   33 E. Minor St., Emmaus, PA 18098

The American Canoeist   The bimonthly publication of the American Canoe Association

Triathlete   Triathlete Productions Inc., 1127 Hamilton St.,
        Allentown, PA 18102

Triathlon   Triathlete Magazine LTD., 1415 3rd St.,
        Santa Monica, CA 90401

Triathlon Times   Tri-Fed, Box 1010,
        Colorado Springs, CO 80901

Books

Multi-sport

Bloch, Godon   *Cross-Training* — Simon & Schuster, 1992
Forsythe, Kenneth   *Athletics For Life* — Simon & Schuster
Gross, Albert   *Endurance* — Dodd, Mead, & Co. 1986
Mangi, Richard   *Sports Fitness And Training* — Pantheon
Scott, Dave   *Triathlon Training* — Simon & Schuster, 1986
  (Excellent Section On Weight Training)
Sleamaker, Rob   *Serious Training For Serious Athletes*
                        Human Kinetics/Leisure Press

Canoeing & Canoe Racing

Birkby, Robert   *Learn How To Canoe In One Day*
                        Stackpole Books, 1990
Evans, Eric & John Burton   *Whitewater Racing*, 1980
Harrison, Dave   *Sports Illustrated Canoeing Skills For The
                Serious Paddler* — NAL, 1988
Harrison, Dave and Judy   *Canoeing with Children* — ICS
Heese, Fred   *Canoe Racing* — Contemporary Books, 1979
Jacobson, Cliff   *Canoeing: The Basic Essentials* — ICS, 1988
Jacobson, Cliff   *Canoeing Wild Rivers* — ICS Books, 1989
Mason, Bill   *Path Of The Paddle* — Van Nostrand Reinhold
Penny, Richard   *The Whitewater Sourcebook*
                Menasha Ridge Press, 1989

Cycling

Borysewicz, Edward   *Bicycle Road Racing* — Vitesse Press
Lemond, Greg   *Greg Lemond's Complete Book of Cycling*
Perigee Books, 1990
Matheney, Fred   *Beginning Bicycle Racing* — Vitesse Press
Roy, Karen   *Fit and Fast: How to Be a Better Cyclist*
Vitesse Press
Schubert, John   *Richard's Cycling For Fitness*
Ballantine, 1987
Woodward, Bob   *Mountain Biking*
Sports Illustrated Books, 1991

Cross Country Skiing

Brady, Michael   *Cross-Country Ski Gear*
The Mountaineers, 1987
Borowski, Lee   *Ski Faster, Easier* — Leisure Press, 1986
Caldwell, John   *The New Cross-Country Ski Book 8th ed.*
The Stephen Greene Press, 1988
Evans, Eric   *Mental Toughness Training For Cross-Country
Skiing* — The Stephen Greene Press, 1990
Gillette, Ned and Dostal, John   *Cross Country Skiing*
The Mountaineers, 1988
Mansfield, Dick   *Skating On Skis* — Acorn Publishing, 1988
Morton, John   *Don't Look Back* — Stackpole Books, 1992

Nutrition

Clark, Nancy   *Nancy Clark's Nutrition Guidebook: Eating To
Fuel Your Active Lifestyle* — Leisure Press, 1990
Coleman, Ellen   *Eating For Endurance*
Bull Publishing, 1988

Strength Training

Baechle, Thomas & Barney Groves   *Weight Training*
Leisure Press, 1992
Bryzcki, Matt   *Practical Approach To Strength Training*
Masters Press, 1989
Matheney, Fred   *Weight Training for Cyclists*
Vitesse Press, 1987
Pearl, Bill & Gary Moran   *Getting Stronger*
Shelter Publications, 1986
Sharkey, Brian J.   *Training For Cross Country Ski Racing*
Human Kinetics, 1984
Sprague, Ken & Bill Reynolds   *The Gold's Gym Book Of Bodybuilding* — Contemporary Books, 1983

Videos

Fries, Mike & Tanna   *Long Distance Canoe Racing* — Clear advice on technique and training for successful canoe racing.

Heed, Peter   *The General Clinton* — Action highlights of the 1989 General Clinton Race with expert narration and motivating music.

U.S. Canoe Association   *Canoeing* — An introduction to quiet water paddling.

National Organizations

American Canoe Association
8580 Cinderbed Road
Suite 1900
P.O. Box 1190
Newington, VA 22122

American Whitewater Affiliation
P.O. Box 85
Phoenicia, NY 12464

National Organization of River Sports
314 N. 20th St.
P.O. Box 6847
Colorado Springs, CO 80934

Tri-Fed
P.O. Box 15820
Colorado Springs, CO 80935

U. S. Canoe Association
Jim Mack, Executive Director
606 Ross Street
Middletown, OH 45044

Canoe Clubs

Arkansas

Have Paddle Will Travel Canoe Club
Clifton Rickey
Rt 6, Box 40
Pocahontas, AR 72455

Connecticut

Connecticut Canoe Racing Association
Earle Roberts
785 Bow Lane
Middletown, CT 06457

Columbia Canoe Club
Sue Audette
41 Pinewoods Lane
Mansfield Center, CT 06250

Quinnipiac River Watershed Association
Sarah Hincks
99 Colony St.
Meriden, CT 06450

Florida

Florida Competition Paddlers
Harold Owens
P.O. Box 152
Valpariso, FL 32580

Illinois

Illinois Paddling Council
Jeff Palmquist
24 Roosevelt St.
St. Charles, IL 60174

Lincoln Park Boat Club
2451 N. Lawndale Ave.
Chicago, IL 60647

Pontiac Paddlers
RR 4, Box 30
Pontiac, IL 61764

St. Charles Canoe Club
24 Roosevelt St.
St. Charles, IL 60174

Indiana

Wildcat Canoe Club
Carmen Dickson
P.O. Box 6232
Kokomo, IN 46904

Kentucky

Elkhorn Paddlers
Scott Handle
934 Brookhaven Drive
Frankfort,KY 40601

Maine

Maine Canoe and Kayak Club
P.O. Box 366
Orono, ME 04473

Massachusetts

Birch Hill Paddlers
P.O. Box 84
Winchendon, MA 01475

Connecticut River Canoe Racers
Frank Stasz
126 Edwards Road
Westhampton, MA 01027

Rat Pack Paddlers, Inc.
P.O. Box 372
Athol, MA 01331

River Runners Canoe Club
44 Pine Hill St.
E. Taunton, MA

Westfield Wildwater Canoe Club
Ingell Road
Chester, MA 01011

Michigan

Lansing Oar & Paddle Club
304 Gunson
East Lansing, MI 48823

Michigan Canoe Racing Association
516 Giles Ave.
Blissfield, MI 49228

Minnesota

Minnesota Canoe Association Inc.
P.O. Box 13567 Dinkytown Sta.
Minneapolis, MN 55414

New Hampshire

River Barn Canoe Club
Peter Heed
RR 1, Box 258A
Westmoreland, NH 03467

New Jersey

Hackensack River Canoe Club
Karen Siletti
P.O. Box 369
Bogota, NJ 07603

Wanda Canoe Club
John Ponticorvo
802 Prospect Ave.
Ridgefield, NJ 07657

New York

Heuvelton Canoe Club
Howard Friot
7 York St.
Heuvelton, NY 13654

New York Canoe Racing Association
John Ayer
2145 East Lake Road
Skaneateles, NY 13152

Northern New York Paddlers
Jim Adams
1007 Tomahawk Trail
Scotia, NY 12302

Onondaga Canoe Club
P.O. Box 2501
Liverpool, NY 13089

Tenandeho Canoe Association
John Erano
718 B Bruno Road
Clifton Park, NY 12065

Upper Susquehanna P & P
Jeff Shultis
RD 1, Box 207D
Otego, NY 13825

Ohio

Dayton Canoe Club
Frank Raley
1020 Riverside Drive
Dayton, OH 45405

Hoosier Canoe Club
1150 Mopac Ct.
Indianapolis, IN 46217

Keel Haulers Canoe Club
Hank Annable
435 West College St.
Oberlin, OH 44074

Ohio Historical Canoe Association
Paul Wood
914 June St.
Fremont, OH 43420

Scenic Scioto Canoe Club
Mike Doyle
1720 Coles Blvd
Portsmouth, OH 45662

Toledo River Gang
Michael Sidell
626 Louisiana Ave.
Perrysburg, OH 43551

Trumbull Canoe Trails, Inc.
Preston Foster
P.O. Box 1390
Warren, OH 44482

Pennsylvania

Keystone River Runners
RD #6, Box 359
Indiana, PA 15701

P.A.C.K.
Jay Behling
917 Pine Hill Road
Lititz, PA 17543

Rhode Island

Rhode Island Canoe Association
193 Pettaconsett Ave.
Warwick, RI 02888

Texas

Texas Canoe Racing Association
139 Park Drive South
Kyle, TX 78640

Washington

Seattle Canoe Club
3047 NW 62nd St.
Seattle, WA 98107

Spokane Canoe & Kayak Club
P.O. Box 819
Spokane, WA 99210

Wenatchee Outdoor Club
1124 Fuller St.
Wenatchee, WA 98801

Wisconsin

Wisconsin Canoe Association
Neil Weisner-Hanks
12455 N. Wauwatosa Rd.
Mequon, WI 53092

Index

ORDER FORM

Title	U.S. Price
[ ] *Canoe Racing*	$14.95
[ ] *Vermont Mountain Biking*	$10.95
[ ] *Skating on Skis*	$9.95
[ ] *Runner's Guide To Cross Country Skiing*	$10.95

We encourage you to buy Acorn books at a book or sports shop. Our titles are available from our book trade distributor, The Countryman Press, as well as many outdoor sports stores. If your local shop is not willing to order the books you want, you can order directly from us. When ordering from Acorn Publishing, prepayment or credit card number and expiration date are required. Please include the price of the book plus postage and handling ($2.50 for the first book, $1.00 for each additional book) as well as sales tax for New York mailing addresses.

Telephone Orders:
(315) 689-7072 — leave a message with name and address, Visa or MC number, and order.

Postal Orders: Acorn Publishing
             Box 7067C, Syracuse, New York 13261

Ordered by (Name) _____

Shipping Address _____

City _____ **State** _____ **Zip** _____

Telephone (   ) _____